Also by Christopher Hitchens

Letters to a Young Contrarian

The Trial of Henry Kissinger

Unacknowledged Legislation: Writers in the Public Sphere

No One Left to Lie To: The Values of the Worst Family

The Missionary Position: Mother Theresa in Theory and Practice

For the Sake of Argument: Essays and Minority Reports

The Monarchy

Blood, Class, and Nostalgia: Anglo-American Ironies

Prepared for the Worst: Selected Essays and Minority Reports

Hostage to History: Cyprus from the Ottomans to Kissinger

Cyprus

Why Orwell Matters

Why Orwell Matters

Christopher Hitchens

BASIC
BOOKS

A Member of the Perseus Books Group

Published by Basic Books,
A Member of the Perseus Books Group

The author and publisher would like to thank Harcourt for permission to
quote from the works of George Orwell; Random House Inc for permission
to quote from W. H. Auden's "September 1, 1939"; Curtis Brown Ltd for
permission to quote from W. H. Auden's "Spain"; and Farrar, Straus and
Giroux for permission to quote from Philip Larkin's "Going, Going."

Designed by Trish Wilkinson

Library of Congress Cataloging-in-Publication Data
Hitchens, Christopher.
    Why Orwell matters / by Christopher Hitchens.
        p.   cm.
ISBN 0-465-03049-1 (alk. paper)
1. Orwell, George, 1903–1950—Criticism and interpretation.   I. Title.
PR6029.R8 Z664 2002
828'.91209—dc21   2002008035

02 03 04 / 10 9 8 7 6 5 4 3 2

Dedicated by permission:
To Robert Conquest — premature anti-fascist,
premature anti-Stalinist, poet and mentor, and
founder of 'the united front against bullshit'.

But genius, and even great talent, springs less from seeds of intellect and social refinement superior to those of other people than from the faculty of transforming and transposing them. To heat a liquid with an electric lamp requires not the strongest lamp possible, but one of which the current can cease to illuminate, can be diverted so as to give heat instead of light. To mount the skies it is not necessary to have the most powerful of motors, one must have a motor which, instead of continuing to run along the earth's surface, intersecting with a vertical line the horizontal which it began by following, is capable of converting its speed into lifting power. Similarly, the men who produce works of genius are not those who live in the most delicate atmosphere, whose conversation is the most brilliant or their culture the most extensive, but those who have had the power, ceasing suddenly to live only for themselves, to transform their personality into a sort of mirror, in such a way that their life, however mediocre it may be socially and even, in a sense, intellectually, is reflected by it, genius consisting in reflecting power and not in the intrinsic quality of the scene reflected.

MARCEL PROUST: *Within a Budding Grove*

Contents

Acknowledgements

My thanks are due first to the Reverend Peter Collingwood, my old English master, who first set me *Animal Farm* as a text and who allowed me to show him my work, late, as an off-the-subject comparison with *Darkness at Noon*: the first decent essay I ever wrote.

The late Claud Cockburn, one of the most generous and charming men I have ever encountered, exposed me to the anti-Orwellian view of the Spanish War and other matters when I was twenty years old, and very patiently taught me more then he probably suspected about how to argue dialectically. These pages are a considered abuse of his unfailing hospitality.

The late Peter Sedgwick — whose name is still a talisman on the noble remnant of the libertarian Left — helped me to develop the puny sinews with which I combated the Cockburn school. He also helped me to recognize a certain 'Orwellianism' as a thread of Ariadne in the writing of our time.

Stephen Schwartz and Ronald Radosh both showed me work in progress from their study of the Soviet archives on Orwell, and I am boundlessly grateful to them as well as to their colleagues and co-authors Victor Alba and Mary Habeck. *Magna est veritas, et prevaelabit.*

Finally, the achievement of Professor Peter Davison, in erecting his majestic edifice of Orwell's entire and un-Bowdlerized life-work, is something more than a Herculean editing or a Boswellian tribute. It is a project of commingled objectivity and love, and thus a great monument to its subject. My own little book is one of the first to be composed in its fully measured shadow, as all the successor and superior theses will now have to be.

Christopher Hitchens
Washington D.C., 4 February 2002

Introduction: The Figure

Moral and mental glaciers melting slightly
Betray the influence of his warm intent.
Because he taught us what the actual meant
The vicious winter grips its prey less tightly.

Not all were grateful for his help, one finds,
For how they hated him, who huddled with
The comfort of a quick remedial myth
Against the cold world and their colder minds.

We die of words. For touchstones he restored
The real person, real event or thing;
— And thus we see not war but suffering
As the conjunction to be most abhorred.

He shared with a great world, for greater ends,
That honesty, a curious cunning virtue
You share with just the few who don't desert you.
A dozen writers, half-a-dozen friends.

A moral genius. And truth-seeking brings
Sometimes a silliness we view askance,
Like Darwin playing his bassoon to plants;
He too had lapses, but he claimed no wings.

While those who drown a truth's empiric part
In dithyramb or dogma turn frenetic;
— Than whom no writer could be less poetic
He left this lesson for all verse, all art.

ROBERT CONQUEST: 'GEORGE ORWELL' (1969)

The stanzas above were written in a glacial time, and refer back to a period of almost polar frigidity — the 'midnight of the century' reviewed through the optic of the Cold War, with the additional prospect of a 'nuclear winter' never remote enough to be dismissed. Yet the chilliness of the opening is at once redeemed by a friendly gleam, and this gleam is renewed through the subsequent glow of friendship until it suffuses the closing lines with something almost like fire.

It's an open question as to whether or not integrity and honesty are cold or hot virtues, and England can be a dank place in which to locate the question. 'Wintry Conscience of a Generation' was Jeffrey Meyers's subtitle for his 2000 Orwell biography — the phrase itself being annexed from the luke-warm pages of V. S. Pritchett. Orwell's own work is much pre-occupied with the demoralizing effects of the freezing point, and not entirely free from the ancestral belief that a cold plunge is a good thing. But this gaunt and aloof person under-went his two crucial epiphanies in the torrid and sultry cli-mates of Burma and Catalonia; and his work in its smuggled form was later to kindle a spark in the Siberias of the world, warming the hearts of shivering Poles and Ukrainians and helping to melt the permafrost of Stalinism. If Lenin had not uttered the maxim 'the heart on fire and the brain on ice', it might have suited Orwell, whose passion and generosity were rivalled only by his detachment and reserve.

Sir Victor Pritchett, as he later became, was among many to have configured Orwell as among the 'saints', albeit a sec-ular member of that communion. Again we are confronted with spareness and the spectre of self-denial, instead of with the profane and humorous writer who said — of Mahatma Gandhi — that saints are always to be adjudged guilty until proven innocent. Speaking of another celebrated supposed Puritan, Thomas Carlyle wrote of his Cromwell that he had had to drag him out from under a mound of dead logs and offal before being able to set him up as a figure worthy of bi-ography. This is not a biography, but I sometimes feel as if George Orwell requires extricating from a pile of saccharine tablets and moist hankies; an object of sickly veneration and sentimental overpraise, employed to stultify schoolchildren with his insufferable rightness and purity. This kind of trib-ute is often of the Rochefoucauldian type, suggestive of the payoff made by vice to virtue; and also of the tricks played by an uneasy conscience. (It was Pritchett, after all, who had cheaply denounced Orwell's dangerously truthful despatches from Barcelona by writing in 1938 that 'there are many strong arguments for keeping creative writers out of politics and Mr George Orwell is one of them'.)

There were very many 'creative writers' with high political profiles in the period that is covered by the years between *Down and Out in Paris and London* (1933) and *Nineteen Eighty-Four* (1949). If we agree to confine ourselves to the English-speaking world, we find George Bernard Shaw, H. G. Wells, J. B. Priestley and Ernest Hemingway as only the foremost. And of course there were the poets — the group collected under the doggerel name 'MacSpaunday' which symbolizes Louis MacNeice, Stephen Spender, W. H. Auden and Cecil Day Lewis. (The portmanteau name omits that of their mentor Edward Upward, about whom Orwell also wrote.) It is fairly safe to say, however, that the political statements made by these men would not bear reprinting today. Some of their pronouncements were stupid or sinister; some were just silly or credulous or flippant. However, and by way of bold contrast, it has lately proved possible to reprint every single letter, book review and essay composed by Orwell without exposing him to any embarrassment. (There is one arguable exception to this verdict, which I intend to discuss separately.)

It would be too simple to say that the gentlemen mentioned above, along with many others in the business of mere journalism, were susceptible to the lures and enticements offered by power while Orwell was not. But it would be true to say that they could expect to see their work in print while he was never able to compose anything with the same confidence in having it published. Thus, his life as a writer was in two important senses a constant struggle: first for the principles he espoused and second for the right to witness to them. He would appear never to have diluted his opinions in the hope of seeing his byline disseminated to the paying customers; this alone is a clue to why he still matters.

However, the image of the drudge in the garret, who takes his failure as a sign of his high principle, is an over-familiar one, which Orwell lampooned with some thorough-ness in his novel *Keep the Aspidistra Flying*. His importance to the century just past, and therefore his status as a figure in history as well as in literature, derives from the extraordinary salience of the subjects he 'took on', and stayed with, and never abandoned. As a consequence, we commonly use the term 'Orwellian' in one of two ways. To describe a state of af-fairs as 'Orwellian' is to imply crushing tyranny and fear and conformism. To describe a piece of writing as 'Orwellian' is to recognize that human resistance to these terrors is un-quenchable. Not bad for one short lifetime.

The three great subjects of the twentieth century were imperialism, fascism and Stalinism. It would be trite to say that these 'issues' are only of historical interest to ourselves; they have bequeathed the whole shape and tone of our era. Most of the intellectual class were fatally compromised by accommodation with one or other of these man-made structures of inhumanity, and some by more than one. (Sid-ney Webb, co-author with his wife Beatrice of the notorious volume *Soviet Russia: A New Civilisation?*, which in its second edition dropped the question mark just in time to coincide with the Great Purges, became Lord Passfield under Ramsay MacDonald's Labour government of 1929, and in that capacity acted as an exceptionally repressive and pompous Colonial Secretary. George Bernard Shaw managed to be stupidly lenient about both Stalin and Mussolini.)

Orwell's decision to repudiate the unthinking imperialism that had been his family's meal ticket (his father was an executive in the degrading opium trade between British India and China) may be represented as Oedipal by those critics who prefer such avenues of inquiry. But it was very thoroughgoing and, for its time, very advanced. It also coloured everything he subsequently wrote. Not only is it strongly present in one of his very first published articles — a review of the way in which British tariffs were underdeveloping Burma, written for the French paper *Le Progrès Civique* in 1929 — but it pervades his first real book, *Down and Out in Paris and London*, and it formed the sub-text of his first contribution to John Lehmann's *New Writing*. Orwell may or may not have felt guilty about the source of his family's income — an image that recurs in his famous portrait of England itself as a family with a conspiracy of silence about its finances — but he undoubtedly came to see the exploitation of the colonies as the dirty secret of the whole enlightened British establishment, both political and cultural. This insight also allowed him to notice certain elements in what Nietzsche had termed the 'master–slave' relationship; his fiction manifests a continual awareness of the awful pleasures and temptations of servility, and many of its most vivid scenes would have been inconceivable without it. Living as we do in the warm afterglow of post-colonialism, and in the complacent appreciation of postcolonial studies, we sometimes forget the debt we owe to this pioneering insistence.

By staying true to what he had won by way of his colonial experience, and to the way he had confirmed it by his sojourns among the empire's internal helots (as one might picture the downtrodden and outcast in the Paris and London of the time), Orwell was in a stronger position to feel viscerally as well as intellectually about the modernist empires of Nazism and Stalinism. Among many other things, of which an educated sympathy for victims and especially racial victims was only one, he had grown sensitive to intellectual hypocrisy and was well-tuned to pick up the invariably creepy noises which it gives off. He was already an old India hand, in other words, when it came to detecting corrupt or euphemistic excuses for undeserved and unchecked power.

His polemics against fascism are, oddly enough, not among his best or best-remembered work. He seems to have taken it for granted that the 'theories' of Hitler and Mussolini and Franco were the distillation of everything that was most hateful and false in the society he already knew; a kind of satanic summa of military arrogance, racist solipsism, schoolyard bullying and capitalist greed. His one especial insight was to notice the frequent collusion of the Roman Catholic Church and of Catholic intellectuals with this saturnalia of wickedness and stupidity; he alludes to it again and again. As I write, the Church and its apologists are only beginning to make their belated amends for this period.

An early volunteer in Spain, Orwell appears to have thought it axiomatic that fascism would mean war (in both senses of the verb 'to mean') and that the battle should be joined (in both senses of that term) as early and decisively as possible. But it was while he was engaged on this front that he came to an understanding of Communism, and began the ten-year combat with its adherents which constitutes, for most people alive today, his intellectual and moral legacy. Without an understanding of his other motives and promptings, however, this legacy is decidedly incomplete.

The first thing to strike any student of Orwell's work and Orwell's life will be its *independence.* Having endured what is often called a 'conventional' English education ('conventional', presumably, because it applies to a microscopic percentage of the population), he did not make the traditional progress to a medieval university, and having chosen the alternative, the colonial service, he abruptly deserted it. From then on, he made his own living in his own way and never had to call any man master. He never enjoyed a stable income, and never had a completely reliable publishing outlet. Uncertain as to whether he was a novelist or not, he added to the richness of English fiction but learned to concentrate on the essay form. Thus, he faced the competing orthodoxies and despotisms of his day with little more than a battered typewriter and a stubborn personality.

The absorbing thing about his independence was that it had to be learned; acquired; won. The evidence of his upbringing and instincts is that he was a natural Tory and even something of a misanthrope. Conor Cruise O'Brien, himself a notable critic of Orwell, once wrote of Edmund Burke that his strength lay in his internal conflicts:

> The contradictions in Burke's position enrich his eloquence, extend its range, deepen its pathos, heighten its fantasy and make possible its strange appeal to 'men of liberal-temper'. On this interpretation, part of the secret of his power to penetrate the processes of the [French] revolution derives from a suppressed sympathy with revolution, combined with an intuitive grasp of the subversive possibilities of *counter*-revolutionary propaganda, as affecting the established order in the land of his birth . . . for him the forces of revolution and counter-revolution exist not only in the world at large but also within himself.

With Orwell, something like the converse applies. He had to suppress his distrust and dislike of the poor, his revulsion from the 'coloured' masses who teemed throughout the empire, his suspicion of Jews, his awkwardness with women and his anti-intellectualism. By teaching himself in theory and practice, some of the teaching being rather pedantic, he became a great humanist. Only one of his inherited prejudices — the shudder generated by homosexuality — appears to have resisted the process of self-mastery. And even that 'perversion' he often represented as a misfortune or deformity created by artificial or cruel conditions; his repugnance —

when he remembered to make this false distinction — was for the 'sin' and not the 'sinner'. (There are occasional hints that unhappy early experience in monastic British institutions may have had a part in this.)

Thus, the Orwell who is regarded by some as being as English as roast beef and warm beer is born in Bengal and publishes his first articles in French. The Orwell who always disliked the Scots and the cult of Scotland makes his home in the (admittedly unpopulated) Hebrides and is one of the few writers of his period to anticipate the potential force of Scottish nationalism. The young Orwell who used to fantasize about driving a bayonet into the guts of a Burmese priest becomes a champion of Burmese independence. The egalitarian and socialist sees simultaneously the fallacy of state-ownership and centralization. The hater of militarism becomes the advocate of a war of national survival. The fastidious and solitary public-schoolboy dosses down with tramps and tarts and forces himself to endure bedbugs and chamberpots and lockups. The extraordinary thing about this *nostalgie de la boue* is that it is undertaken with a humorous self-consciousness and without any tinge of religious abjection or mortification. The foe of jingoism and muscular Christianity is one of the finest writers about patriotic verse and the liturgical tradition.

This creative tension, coupled with a hard-won confidence in his own individual convictions, enabled Orwell to be uncommonly prescient not just about the 'isms' — imperialism, fascism, Stalinism — but about many of the themes and subjects that preoccupy us today. Rereading his collected works, and immersing myself in the vast new material collected by the exemplary labour of Professor Peter Davison, I found myself in the presence of a writer who is still vividly contemporary. Some instances include:

- his work on 'the English question', as well as the related matters of regional nationalism and European integration;
- his views on the importance of language, which anticipated much of what we now debate under the rubric of psychobabble, bureaucratic speech, and 'political correctness';
- his interest in demotic or popular culture, and in what now passes for 'cultural studies';
- his fascination with the problem of objective or verifiable truth — a central problem in the discourse now offered us by post-modern theorists;
- his influence on later fiction, including the so-called 'Angry Young Man' novel;
- his concern with the natural environment and what is now considered as 'green' or 'ecological';
- his acute awareness of the dangers of 'nuclearism' and the nuclear state.

This list is a partial one. There is one outstanding lacuna: his relative indifference to the importance of the United States as an emerging dominant culture. Yet even here, he was able to register some interesting insights and forecasts, and his work found an immediate audience among those American writers

and critics who valued English prose and political honesty.*
Prominent among these was Lionel Trilling, who made two
observations of great acuity about him. The first was to say
that he — Orwell — was a modest man because in many
ways he had much to be modest about:

> If we ask what it is he stands for, what he is the figure of,
> the answer is: the virtue of not being a genius, of fronting
> the world with nothing more than one's simple, direct,
> undeceived intelligence, and a respect for the powers one
> does have, and the work one undertakes to do . . . He is
> not a genius — what a relief! What an encouragement.
> For he communicates to us the sense that what he has
> done, any one of us could do.

This perception is of the first importance, also, in explaining
the sheer hatred of Orwell that is still to be found in some

---

*It still does. In the immediate aftermath of 11 September 2001, when a number
of intellectuals and pseudo-intellectuals affected a sort of neutrality between the
victims of New York and Pennsylvania and Washington and the theocratic fascists of Al Quaeda and the Taliban, a large e-mail circulation was given to this extract from Orwell's May 1945 essay, *Notes on Nationalism*:

> The majority of pacifists either belong to obscure religious sects or are sim-
> ply humanitarians who object to taking life and prefer not to follow their
> thoughts beyond that point. But there is a minority of intellectual pacifists,
> whose real though unacknowledged motive appears to be hatred of western
> democracy and admiration for totalitarianism. Pacifist propaganda usually
> boils down to saying that one side is as bad as the other, but if one looks
> closely at the writings of the younger intellectual pacifists, one finds that
> they do not by any means express impartial disapproval but are directed al-
> most entirely against Britain and the United States . . .

quarters. By living and writing as he did, he discredited the excuse of 'historical context' and the shady alibi that there was, in the circumstances, nothing else that people could have done. In turn, this licenses Professor Trilling's next point, most beautifully stated, where he speculates on the nature of personal integrity:

> Orwell clung with a kind of wry, grim pride to the old ways of the last class that had ruled the old order. He must sometimes have wondered how it came about that he should be praising sportsmanship and gentlemanliness and dutifulness and physical courage. He seems to have thought, and very likely he was right, that they might come in handy as revolutionary virtues . . .

'Facing it —' as Captain MacWhirr says so memorably in Joseph Conrad's 'Typhoon', 'always facing it — that's the way to get through.'

'I knew,' said Orwell in 1946 about his early youth, 'that I had a facility with words and a power of facing unpleasant facts.' Not the ability to face them, you notice, but 'a power of facing'. It's oddly well put. A commissar who realizes that his five-year plan is off-target and that the people detest him or laugh at him may be said, in a base manner, to be confronting an unpleasant fact. So, for that matter, may a priest with 'doubts'. The reaction of such people to unpleasant facts is rarely self-critical; they do not have the 'power of facing'. Their confrontation with the fact takes the form of an evasion; the reaction to the unpleasant discovery is a redoubling of efforts to overcome the obvious. The 'unpleasant facts' that Orwell faced were usually the ones that put his own position or preference to the test.

Though he popularized and dramatized the concept of the all-powerful telescreen, and worked for some years in the radio section of the BBC, Orwell died early and impoverished before the age of austerity gave way to the age of celebrity and mass media. We have no real record of what he sounded like, or of how he would have 'come across' on a TV chat show. Probably this is just as well. His photographs show someone lean but humorous, proud but by no means vain. And yes, as a matter of fact, we do have his voice, and don't seem to have reached a stage where we can say we no longer need it. As for his 'moral genius' — Robert Conquest's phrase, in accidental opposition to Trilling — this may or may not be found in the details.

1

Orwell and Empire

It was once written of George Orwell that by consorting with the unemployed and destitute of England he 'went native in his own country'. The remark is even truer than it appears, as I hope to show, but one should notice for now that the expression 'going native' originated as a term of contempt for white men who cracked under pressure. 'Native' was a colonialist term for wogs or niggers or gyppos; a lazy generalization about subject peoples. Every now and then, a young chap shipped out from home would prove unsuitable, and would take to drink or to siestas or — this being the extreme case — to concubinage with a local woman or boy. The older and steadier officials and businessmen would learn to recognize the symptoms; it was part of their job.

An old radical adage states that the will to command is not as corrupting as the will to obey. We do not know with

absolute certainty what impelled Orwell to abandon the life
of a colonial policeman, but it seems to have involved a version of this same double-edged slogan. The word 'brutalize'
is now employed quite wrongly to mean harsh or cruel treatment meted out by the strong to the weak ('the Russian
army brutalized the Chechens' etc.). But in fact it means
something subtler, namely the coarsening effect that this exercise of cruelty produces in the strong.

'In Moulmein, in Lower Burma,' wrote Orwell at the
opening of his essay 'Shooting an Elephant', 'I was hated by
large numbers of people — the only time in my life that I
have been important enough for this to happen to me. I was
sub-divisional police officer of the town . . .' It's a nice coincidence that Moulmein is featured in the first line of Rudyard Kipling's wonderful and nonsensical poem of imperial
nostalgia 'Mandalay' ('By the old Moulmein Pagoda, lookin'
eastward to the sea,/ There's a Burma girl a-settin', an' I
know she thinks o' me'). But there was little romance in Orwell's account of the place; he clearly worried at some level
that the experience of being a cop was turning him into a
sadist or an automaton. In 'A Hanging' he describes the dis-
mal futility of an execution and the terrible false jocularity of
the gallows humour, his honesty forcing him to confess that
he had joined in the empty laughter. In 'Shooting an Elephant' he gives a sketchy account of the sordid side of the
colonial mentality:

> I had already made up my mind that imperialism was an
> evil thing and the sooner I chucked up my job and got

out of it the better. Theoretically — and secretly, of course — I was all for the Burmese and all against their oppressors, the British. As for the job I was doing, I hated it more bitterly than I can perhaps make clear. In a job like that you see the dirty work of Empire at close quarters. The wretched prisoners huddling in the stinking cages of the lock-ups, the grey, cowed faces of the long-term convicts, the scarred buttocks of the men who had been flogged with bamboos — all these oppressed me with an intolerable sense of guilt.

This private animosity and confusion did not by any means translate into sympathy for the 'natives', who made Orwell's job a misery whenever they felt strong enough, and it is at least pardonable to speculate that he resigned the service as abruptly as he did because of the fear that he might indeed get too used to the contradiction. In the later novel *Burmese Days,* the central character Flory (who anticipates the sweltering banana-republic cosmos of Graham Greene by a few years) is compelled to live in a 'stifling, stultifying world . . . in which every word and every thought is censored . . . Free speech is unthinkable . . . the secrecy of your revolt poisons you like a secret disease. Your whole life is a life of lies.' That this is a strong prefiguration of the mentality of Winston Smith in *Nineteen Eighty-Four* will be obvious; that it is no exaggeration is confirmed by the memoir of Orwell's friend and contemporary Christopher Hollis, who visited him in Burma in 1925 and discovered him mouthing the platitudes of law-and-order: 'He was at pains to be the imperial policeman, explaining that

these theories of punishment and no beating were all very well
at public schools, but that they did not work with the
Burmese . . . '

Four years later, in the pages of *Le Progrès Civique* in Paris, a
certain 'E. A. Blair' contributed an essay in French entitled
*'Comment on exploite un peuple: L'Empire britannique en Bir-
manie'* ('How a Nation is Exploited: The British Empire in
Burma'). The article could justly be described as workman-
like; it commences with a careful account of the country's to-
pography and demography and proceeds to a meticulous examination of the way the colonial power fleeces the Burmese
of their natural resources and the fruits of their labour. It is,
in all essentials, a study in deliberate underdevelopment and
the means by which raw materials are used to finance another country's industrial progress. But one may also notice
the emergence of another trope: the author's keen and sad
interest in the passivity and docility of the victims, who
know little or nothing of the wider mercantile world from
which their nation is being excluded.

This article was the latest in a series of occasional pieces
written by 'E. A. Blair' — his Etonian and Burma Police
name, not to be abandoned for Orwell until 1933 and the
publication of *Down and Out* — for the Parisian radical
press. The very first such essay was a study of censorship in
England, published by Henri Barbusse's weekly *Monde,* a
sort of cultural-literary front-publication of the French
Communist Party. This article, also, was a thorough study of

a given question which also contained a psychically interesting undertone. The British authorities, wrote 'E. A. Blair',
were not so much censorious as prudish, and had not felt the
necessity for censorship until the rise of the Protestant and
capitalist ethic. A rather ordinary point even for its time, but
it did presage a lifelong interest in the relationship between
power and sexual repression (a theme not absent from Flory's
own sweaty reflections in *Burmese Days*).

It is never pointed out that Orwell's journals from the
lower depths, his narratives of dish-washing in Paris and
hop-picking and tramping in England, also show a sensitiv-
ity to what might be called 'the native question'. Algerian
and Moroccan and other French-African characters are a
strong element in his account of the Parisian underclass,
while back at home and hanging about between Wapping
and Whitechapel the author noticed that: 'The East London
women are pretty (it is the mixture of blood, perhaps), and
Limehouse was sprinkled with Orientals — Chinamen,
Chittagonian lascars, Dravidians selling silk scarves, even a
few Sikhs, come goodness knows how.' Not every young English freelance scribbler of twenty-eight or so would have
been able to tell a Dravidian from a Sikh, let alone give a
name to the home-port of the lascars.

In May 1936, Orwell wrote to his agent, Leonard Moore,
in order to discuss, among other matters, a proposal from an
American producer to make a dramatized version of *Burmese
Days*. 'If this project comes to anything,' he said, 'I would
suggest the title "Black Man's Burden."' I do not know if this
is the earliest version of a joke on Kipling that has been

played many times since — most recently in Basil Davidson's superb histories of pre-colonial Africa — but it exemplifies Orwell's ambivalence about the poet and his lack of ambivalence about the subject; an indication of his lifelong refusal to judge literature by a politicized standard.

There seems no doubt that his insight into the colonial mentality informed Orwell's dislike of the class system at home and also of fascism, which he regarded as an extreme form of class rule (albeit expressed paradoxically through a socialistic ideology). In 1940 he began an essay by recalling an incident of odious brutality he had witnessed at Colombo harbour on his first day in Asia. A white policeman had delivered a savage kick to a local coolie, eliciting general murmurs of approbation from the onlooking British passengers:

> That was nearly twenty years ago. Are things of this kind still happening in India? I should say that they probably are, but that they are happening less and less frequently. On the other hand it is tolerably certain that at this moment a German somewhere or other is kicking a Pole. It is quite certain that a German somewhere or other is kicking a Jew. And it is also certain (*vide* the German newspapers) that German farmers are being sentenced to terms of imprisonment for showing 'culpable kindness' to the Polish prisoners working for them. For the sinister development of the past twenty years has been the spread of racialism to the soil of Europe itself . . . racialism is something totally different. It is the invention not of conquered nations but of conquering nations. It is a way of pushing exploitation

beyond the point that is normally possible, by pretending that the exploited *are not human beings.*

Nearly all aristocracies having real power have depended on a difference of race, Norman rules over Saxon, German over Slav, Englishman over Irishman, white man over black man, and so on and so forth. There are traces of the Norman predominance in our own language to this day. And it is much easier for the aristocrat to be ruthless if he imagines that the serf is different from himself in blood and bone. Hence the tendency to exaggerate race-differences, the current rubbish about shapes of skulls, colour of eyes, blood-counts etc., etc. In Burma I have listened to racial theories which were less brutal than Hitler's theories about the Jews, but certainly not less idiotic.

Not long ago, I was reading some essays by the late C. Vann Woodward, the great American academic chronicler of the Old South. He had once investigated the parallels between American slavery and Russian serfdom, and found not entirely to his surprise that the Russian aristocrats did hold the belief that serfs were a lower order of being. (Their bones, for example, were believed to be black . . .)

During this period, Orwell was following developments in North Africa very intently, and wishing that the British and French governments would have the imagination to intervene in Spanish Morocco and help to establish an independent anti-Franco regime there, headed by exiled Spanish republicans. In a form somewhat adapted to wartime conditions, this had been the formula proposed by the Spanish left-revolutionaries

during the Civil War. They favoured Moroccan independence
on principle, but also felt that, since Franco's military-fascist re-
bellion had originally been raised in Morocco, such a policy
stood a good chance of taking him in the rear. The official Left,
especially the Stalinists, had opposed the strategy on the
grounds that it might offend the British and French authorities
who had interests of their own in North Africa. Not content
with this pusillanimity, they had made chauvinistic propaganda
against the barbaric 'Moors' who fought as levies in Franco's
Catholic-run crusade. Though the Moors were credited with
many atrocities, and it was felt particularly important on the republican side not to be taken prisoner by them, there is no trace
in Orwell's writing of any xenophobic or — as we would now
write the term — racist attitude towards Spain's colonial subjects. (Indeed, he spent a season or two composing a novel in
Morocco just before the outbreak of the Second World War,
and wrote a journal highly sympathetic to its inhabitants, including the Jews and the Berbers.)

His rooted opposition to imperialism is a strong and consistent theme throughout all his writings. It could take contra-
dictory forms — he was fond of Kipling's line about 'making
mock of uniforms that guard you while you sleep', because he
thought it captured the hypocrisy of much well-fed liberalism
— but in general he insisted that the whole colonial 'racket'
was corrupting to the British and degrading to the colonized.
Even during the years of the Second World War, when there
was a dominant don't-rock-the-boat mentality and a great
pressure to close ranks against the common foe, Orwell upheld the view that the war should involve decolonization. The
'Searchlight' pamphlet series, of which he was an originator,

included his demand (in *The Lion and the Unicorn*) that India be promoted from colony to full and independent ally, and also his introduction to Joyce Cary's booklet *African Freedom*. In his work in the Indian Service of the BBC, where he struggled, as he put it, to keep 'our little corner' of the airwaves clean, he worked alongside declared supporters of independence, including Communists and nationalists.

Actually, he did rather better than keep his corner clean. His radio magazine 'Voice' was a high-standard uncondescending journal of literature and ideas, keeping an audience of educated Indians in touch with the work, and the tones, of E. M. Forster, T. S. Eliot, Stephen Spender, William Empson and Herbert Read. In a series of war commentaries, Orwell stressed the forgotten 'fronts' that made this a World War: the colonial and anti-colonial engagements in Abyssinia, Timor, Madagascar, Java, Morocco and other territories where the claim of the Allies to be on the side of freedom was being put to the test. When invited to broadcast to India using his own name, because of his high reputation in the sub-continent, he replied that he would only do so if his anti-imperialist opinions could be expressed without dilution. In correspondence, he repeatedly attacked the British government's failure of nerve and principle on the central question of Indian self-government, never ceasing to argue that independence was desirable in itself as well as being a sound tactical move in the face of Japanese aggression. He made use of his knowledge of some Asian languages, and kept closely in touch with developments in his beloved Burma.

In 1938, without his knowledge, he had been 'vetted' by the India Office. A liberal editor in India wanted to employ

him as an editorial writer on the Lucknow *Pioneer*, and had
written to the authorities in London seeking their advice. He
received in return a masterpiece of bureaucratic elegance
composed by A. H. Joyce, Director of Information at the
India Office:

> There is no doubt in my mind about his ability as a
> leader-writer, though I think you may have to be pre-
> pared, in view of what I assess to be not merely a deter-
> mined Left Wing, but probably an extremist, outlook,
> plus definite strength of character, for difficulties when
> there is a conflict of views . . .

This tribute to Orwell's 'power of facing' was not released by
the Foreign Office until 1980; there is still a closed section of
the dossier that was kept on him. And it was this same A. H.
Joyce who helped supervise the India broadcasts at the Empire Section of the BBC. Much of Orwell's time was spent
circumventing such surveillance and interference. At one
point he was compelled to advise E. M. Forster not to mention the work of K. S. Shelvankar, on the grounds that his
book had been banned in India. However, not many months
later we find Orwell writing in person to Shelvankar and
asking him to do some broadcasts on the history of fascism
under his own name. A Burmese colleague (from Moulmein)
named M. Myat Tun was severely reprimanded by Joyce for a
broadcast on 'What Trade Unionism Means to the Worker';
Joyce's angry note about the talk suggests that he suspected
Orwell to be the mischief-maker.

There seems no doubt that Orwell made use of his BBC experiences in the writing of *Nineteen Eighty-Four*. The room where the editorial meetings of Eastern Services were held was Room 101 in the Portland Place headquarters, itself one of the likely architectural models for the 'Ministry of Truth' (Minitrue). Moreover, the concept of doublethink and the description of vertiginous changes in political line clearly owe something to Orwell's everyday experience of propaganda. In August 1942, just after the British had interned the leadership of the Congress Party, he wrote the following in his diary:

> Horrabin was broadcasting today, and as always we introduced him as the man who drew the maps for Wells's *Outline of History* and Nehru's *Glimpses of World History*. This had been extensively trailed and advertised beforehand, Horrabin's connection with Nehru naturally being a draw for India. Today the reference to Nehru was cut out from the announcement — N. being in prison and therefore having become Bad.

Orwell often made reference to Churchill's own broadcasts, being caught between an admiration of them and a resistance to their sometimes bombastic tone. He might have been amused to discover what was not revealed until the late 1970s — that many of these exercises in 'Finest Hour' rhetoric were recorded and delivered by Mr Norman Shelley, a 'Children's Hour' actor with a gift for mimicry, who employed one of the smaller studios in the Portland Place HQ. The voice of the Leader was ventriloquized for the masses . . .

An earlier diary entry, this one ostensibly unpolitical, will also strike a chord with readers of *Nineteen Eighty-Four*.

> The only time when one hears people singing in the B.B.C. is in the early morning, between 6 and 8. That is the time when the charwomen are at work. A huge army of them arrives all at the same time. They sit in the reception hall waiting for their brooms to be issued to them and making as much noise as a parrot house, and then they have wonderful choruses, all singing together as they sweep the passages. The place has a quite different atmosphere at this time from what it has later in the day.

And thus the concept of the 'prole' woman, motherly and eternal and enduring, who has the capacity to survive (or to ignore) all the dictates of the Party.

Orwell's sense of irony did not desert him, and was not always turned upon his tiresome political masters. In April 1942 — while he was still officially a 'Good' thing — Nehru gave an address to the Indian people and adapted Kipling's 1914 poem 'For All We Have and Are'. As Orwell told his diary: 'From Nehru's speech today: "Who dies if India live?" How impressed the pinks will be — how they would snigger at "Who dies if England live?"' Unlike some 'pinks', indeed, Orwell never romanticized the victims of colonialism, and was frequently annoyed by the self-centredness and sectarianism of certain Indian militants. He was at pains, instructing or advising some of his Asian colleagues, to tell them not to overlook the plight of the Jews in their broadcasts to Asia. Though never at all an enthusiast for Zionism, he took care to repudiate German and Japanese claims that the attempted rescue of European Jewry was no more than a scheme to colonize Palestine. As far as possible in an atmosphere of state-sponsored patriotism, he insisted on an internationalist stand.

In Paris as a correspondent at the end of the war, he continued to stress what might be termed the 'Third World' dimension of the struggle against fascism. He enthused over the editorial policy of *Libertés,* which was a Parisian left-socialist equivalent of *Tribune* and took a staunch anti-colonial line, and he was among the few to see the significance of General de Gaulle's attempted restoration of French rule in Indo-China. Commenting on this in a despatch for the *Observer,* he wrote:

> Except when something violent happens, the French overseas territories hardly find their way into the French Press. It is only by dipping into quite obscure periodicals that one can learn, for instance, that in Algeria and Morocco the Vichy apparatus is still largely functioning and the local Socialist and Communist Press is fighting for its life against heavily-subsidised newspapers of reactionary tendency . . . It is curious that there is very little awareness here of the strategic dependence of the French Empire on other Powers. Large portions of it would be quite indefensible without American or British help, and Indo-China, in particular, is very unlikely to remain in French possession without the agreement of China as well.

These brief lines could serve as an introduction to what the whole world later came to know as the Vietnam War; within less than a decade the French military role in Vietnam and

Cambodia was supplanted by that of the United States, and Communist China was a co-signer of the Geneva Accords that temporarily divided Vietnam into North and South. The atmosphere of this surreptitious transition from French Indo-China to Americanization was to be well-caught a few years later by Graham Greene in his novel *The Quiet American*. (Orwell had fired a shot across Greene's bows in the *New Yorker* in 1948. Reviewing *The Heart of the Matter*, and finding Major Scobie to be an implausible character both from the theological and matrimonial point of view, he concluded rather feelingly: 'And one might add that if he were the kind of man we are told he is — that is, a man whose chief characteristic is a horror of causing pain — he would not be an officer in a colonial police force.' The Burmese days stayed with him until the end.)

Mary McCarthy, a great admirer of Orwell's, once confessed, in her book *The Writing on the Wall*, that she had always secretly feared something. His unbending anti-Communism, she suspected, would have prevented him from joining her in opposing the American war in Vietnam. (In interviews at the time, both Noam Chomsky and Norman Mailer gave Orwell as authority for their militant anti-war positions.) I once had the honour of telling Ms McCarthy why I thought they were right and she was wrong about this; it seems obvious from the record that Orwell was for decolonization without conditions, and that he saw clearly the imperial-successor role that the United States was ambitious to play. Remaining doubts on this score are also dispelled by a letter he wrote to the Duchess of Atholl in November 1945.

She had invited him to speak on the platform of the League for European Freedom, at a meeting protesting at Communist brutality in Yugoslavia. He responded:

> Certainly what is said on your platforms is more truthful than the lying propaganda to be found in most of the press, but I cannot associate myself with an essentially Conservative body which claims to defend democracy in Europe but has nothing to say about British imperialism. It seems to me that one can only denounce the crimes now being committed in Poland, Jugoslavia etc. if one is equally insistent on ending Britain's unwanted rule in India. I belong to the Left and must work inside it, much as I hate Russian totalitarianism and its poisonous influence in this country.

The Duchess was perhaps naive in writing to Orwell in the first place; he had already written a withering account of a meeting of her League for *Tribune*, in which he reminded readers of her own previous role as an enthusiastic fellow-traveller of the Communists in Spain:

> It is only about seven years since the Duchess — the 'Red Duchess' as she was affectionately nicknamed — was the pet of the *Daily Worker* and lent the considerable weight of her authority to every lie that the Communists happened to be uttering at the moment. Now she is fighting against the monster that she helped to create. I am sure that neither she nor her Communist ex-friends see any moral in this.

At any rate, she was even more naive when she wrote back to him. Taking up his point about India, she instructed Orwell that 'just as I do not think children or young people are ready for a share in self-Government, so I think we have to recognise that there are races in the Empire which are more youthful than our own in these matters, and therefore must be led gradually along the path that leads to self-rule'. The concept of race-childhood had of course been more eloquently expressed by Kipling in his 'White Man's Burden', which spoke of:

> Your new-caught, sullen peoples,
> Half devil and half child.

It is unwise to forget how long this attitude persisted among the British, and how much Orwell fought against it, and how much he learned from doing so.

A year or so later, in 1947, he wrote an indignant attack in *Tribune* on a piece of ignorant populism published in the *Daily Herald*:

> The *Daily Herald* for January 1, 1947, has a headline MEN WHO SPOKE FOR HITLER HERE, and underneath this a photograph of two Indians who are declared to be Brijlal Mukerjee and Anjit Singh, and are described as having come 'from Berlin.' The news column below the photograph goes on to say that 'four Indians who might have been shot as traitors' are staying at a London hotel, and further describes the group of Indians who broadcast over the German radio during the war as 'collaborators.' It is worth looking a bit more closely at these various statements.

To begin with, there are at least two errors of fact, one of them a very serious one. Anjit Singh did not broadcast on the Nazi radio, but only from Italian stations, while the man described as 'Brijlal Mukerjee' is an Indian who has been in England throughout the war and is well-known to myself and many other people in London . . .

Orwell went on to defend the right of Indians to act as 'citizens of an occupied country' even when he disagreed with the specific actions they took, and to distinguish them sharply from the 'collaborators' like Quisling and Laval who had betrayed their own peoples. He closed by pointing out that the 'photograph' of Brijlal Mukerjee was in fact of somebody else, and asked sarcastically if the newspaper would have made such a crass mistake in the case of a white person. 'But since it's only an Indian, a mistake of this kind doesn't matter — so runs the unspoken thought. And this happens not in the *Daily Graphic*, but in Britain's sole Labour newspaper.'

While serving in Asia, Orwell took the trouble to learn Burmese and Hindustani, as well as a more obscure Shaw-Karen tongue of the Burmese hill people. He felt contempt for those British settlers, including members of his own family, who spent a lifetime in the region without acquiring any but a few peremptory words of command for servants. By the same token, he was most intrigued by the number of Indians who had acquired a literary mastery of English, as well as by the small group of writers, Cedric Dover among them, who were of mixed Anglo-Indian parentage. Reviewing a novel entitled *The Sword and The Sickle* by his friend Mulk Raj Anand in July 1942, he told the readers of *Horizon*:

The growth, especially during the last few years, of an English-language Indian literature is a strange phenomenon, and it will have its effect on the post-war world, if not on the outcome of the war itself . . . At present English is to a great extent the official and business language of India: five million Indians are literate in it and millions more speak a debased version of it; there is a huge English-language Indian Press, and the only English magazine devoted wholly to poetry is edited by Indians. On average, too, Indians write and even pronounce English far better than any European race . . .

Having taken his analysis this far, Orwell began to draw back from its implications, speculating that the end of imperial rule would mean the withering of the English faculty in India. (His habitual pessimism likewise convinced him that the broadcasts to India were largely a waste of time, though their impact was larger than he supposed.) However, in 1943 he returned to the subject, this time addressing Anand directly by means of an open letter-cum-review in the pages of *Tribune*: 'The best bridge between Europe and Asia, better than trade or battleships or aeroplanes, is the English language; and I hope that you and Ahmed Ali and the others will continue to write in it, even if it sometimes leads you to be called a "babu" (as you were recently) at one end of the map and a renegade at the other.'

When Salman Rushdie produced his own anthology of Indian writing in English in 1997, co-edited with Elizabeth West, he emphasized the continuing if not increasing vitality of English as a literary medium in the sub-continent and its diaspora. And he, too, got into hot water with some over-enthusiastic patriots 'back home'. But by then, the shelves of every English bookstore were furnished with testimony from Rohinton Mistry, Arundhati Roy, Pankaj Mishra, Hanif Kureishi, Anita Desai, Vikram Seth and many others, including the Polish-born Ruth Prawer Jhabvala (not the only one of the above, incidentally, to keep open the interesting question of quite where 'back home' might be). An earlier generation of British readers had already feasted on Nirad Chaudhuri, R. K. Narayan and (imperishable for some of us) G. V. Desani. In his introduction, written half a century after independence, Rushdie had this to say:

> The prose writing — both fiction and non-fiction — created in this period by Indian writers *working in English*, is proving to be a stronger and more important body of work than most of what has been produced in the 16 'official languages' of India, the so-called 'vernacular languages', during the same time; and, indeed, this new, and still burgeoning, 'Indo-Anglian' literature represents perhaps the most valuable contribution India has yet made to the world of books.

Facing directly the accusation of using a conqueror's language, Rushdie replied calmly but firmly:

> My own mother-tongue, Urdu, the camp-argot of the country's earlier Muslim conquerors, became a naturalised

sub-continental language long ago; and by now that has
happened to English, too. English has become an Indian
language . . . In many parts of South India, people will
prefer to converse with visiting North Indians in English
rather than Hindi, which feels, ironically, more like a colonial language to speakers of Tamil, Kannada or May-
alayam than does English, which has acquired, in the
South, an aura of *lingua franca* cultural neutrality.

In Rushdie's anthology, a short story entitled 'The Liar', by
Mulk Raj Anand, held pride of place. He appeared to have
transcended the 'babu' slander in more than one way.

It might not be too much to say that the clarity and
courage of Orwell's prose, which made him so readily trans-
latable for Poles and Ukrainians, also played a part in making
English a non-imperial lingua franca. In any event, his writings on colonialism are an indissoluble part of his lifelong engagement with the subjects of power and cruelty and force,
and the crude yet subtle relationship between the dominator
and the dominated. Since one of the great developments of
his time and ours is the gradual emancipation of the formerly
colonized world, and its increasing presence through migra-
tion and exile in the lands of the 'West', Orwell can be read as
one of the founders of the discipline of post-colonialism,
as well as one of the literary registers of the historic transition
of Britain from an imperial and monochrome (and paradoxically insular) society to a multicultural and multi-ethnic one.

2

Orwell and the Left

George Orwell spent much of his youth investigating the condition of the working class in England, and not merely in describing it but in tabulating and collating the relevant statistics. (The notebooks and research for *The Road to Wigan Pier* would not have disgraced Friedrich Engels.) When Spain was menaced by fascism he was among the first to shoulder a rifle and feel the weight of a pack. He helped keep alive the socialist press in England through many unpropitious years. His commitment to the egalitarian ideal was so thorough that it can seem positively old-fashioned. And in the anti-imperialist tradition his name can safely be mentioned alongside those of E. D. Morel, R. B. Cunninghame-Grahame and Wilfred Scawen Blunt; men whose 'magnanimous indignation' (Joseph Conrad's phrase for his friend

Cunninghame-Grahame) placed them on the side of the oppressed and made them — like Orwell's contemporary and
colleague Fenner Brockway — more famous in other countries than they ever were in their 'own'.

Yet on the political and cultural Left, the very name of
Orwell is enough to evoke a shiver of revulsion. Let me supply a few examples:

> *Inside the Whale* must itself be read as an apology for qui-
> etism . . . Orwell is like a man who is raw all down one
> side and numb on the other. He is sensitive — sometimes
> obsessionally so — to the least insincerity upon his left,
> but the inhumanity of the right rarely provoked him to a
> paragraph of polemic . . . Who would suppose, from Or-
> well's indiscriminate rejection, that there were many
> Communists from Tom Wintringham to Ralph Fox who
> shared his criticisms of orthodoxy? . . . Orwell found con-
> firmation of his 'world-process' in the *Managerial Revolu-
> tion* of the ex-Trotskyist, James Burnham; and in the writ-
> ings of the ex-Communist, Arthur Koestler, he found
> confirmation of the corruption of human motive. By
> 1946 politics appeared to him as 'a mass of lies, evasions,
> folly, hatred and schizophrenia' (*Politics and the English
> Language*). *1984* was the product not of one mind, but of
> a culture. (E. P. Thompson: 'Outside the Whale' (1960))

It would also be wrong to go any further without discussing the senses in which Orwell uses the term 'politics'.
Six years after 'Inside the Whale', in the essay 'Politics and

the English Language' (1946), he wrote: 'In our age there is no such thing as "keeping out of politics". All issues are political issues, and politics itself is a mass of lies, evasions, folly, hatred and schizophrenia' . . . The quietist option, the exhortation to submit to events, is an intrinsically conservative one. When intellectuals and artists withdraw from the fray, politicians feel safer. Once, the right and left in Britain used to argue about who 'owned' Orwell. In those days both sides wanted him; and, as Raymond Williams has said, the tug-of-war did his memory little honour. I have no wish to reopen these old hostilities; but the truth cannot be avoided, and the truth is that passivity always serves the interests of the status quo, of the people already at the top of the heap, and the Orwell of 'Inside the Whale' and *Nineteen Eighty-Four* is advocating ideas that can only be of service to our masters. (Salman Rushdie: 'Outside the Whale' [1984])

Orwell's sustained political writing career coincides not with his down-and-out years, nor with his brief interest in the concrete experience of imperialism (*Burmese Days*), but with his readmission to and subsequent residence inside bourgeois life. Politics was something he observed, albeit as an honest partisan, from the comforts of bookselling, marriage, friendship with other writers (not by any means with the radicals used as material for *The Road to Wigan Pier* and *Homage to Catalonia*, then dropped), dealing with publishers and literary agents . . . Out of this style has grown the eye-witness, seemingly

opinion-less politics — along with its strength and weakness — of contemporary Western journalism. When they
are on the rampage, you show Asiatic and African mobs
rampaging: an obviously disturbing scene presented by an
obviously unconcerned reporter who is beyond Left piety
or right-wing cant. But are such events only events when
they are shown through the eyes of the decent reporter?
Must we inevitably forget the complex reality that produced the event just so that we can experience concern at
mob violence? Is there to be no remarking of the power
that put the reporter or analyst there in the first place and
made it possible to represent the world as a function of
comfortable concern? (Edward Said: 'Tourism Among the
Dogs' [1980])

It would be dangerous to blind ourselves to the fact
that in the West millions of people may be inclined, in
their anguish and fear, to flee from their own responsibility
for mankind's destiny and to vent their anger and despair
on the giant Bogy-cum-Scapegoat which Orwell's *1984*
has done so much to place before their eyes. (Isaac
Deutscher: '"1984" — The Mysticism of Cruelty' [1955])

Orwell prepared the orthodox political beliefs of a
generation . . . By viewing the struggle as one between
only a few people over the heads of an apathetic mass, Orwell created the conditions for defeat and despair. (Raymond Williams: *George Orwell* [1971])

Orwell seldom wrote about foreigners, except sociolog-
ically, and then in a hit-or-miss fashion otherwise unusual
with him; he very rarely mentions a foreign writer and has
an excessive dislike of foreign words; although he con-
demns imperialism he dislikes its victims even more . . . Is
it fantastic to see in Orwell's *1984* the reflection of a feeling
that a world in which the pre-1914 British way of life had
totally passed away must necessarily be a dehumanized
world? And is it altogether wrong to see the inhabitants of
Animal Farm as having points in common, not merely with
Soviet Russians, but also with Kipling's lesser breeds generally, as well as with Flory's Burmese who, once the relative
decencies of the Raj are gone, must inevitably fall under the
obscene domination of their own kind? (Conor Cruise
O'Brien: 'Orwell Looks at the World' [1961])

The above citations are only a sample, but by no means an
unrepresentative one, of what might be offered, by way of il-
lustrating the sheer ill will and bad faith and intellectual confusion that appear to ignite spontaneously when Orwell's
name is mentioned in some quarters. Or perhaps not so
spontaneously; it can be seen at a glance that the various authors attribute immense potency to Orwell, that they make
the common mistake of blaming him for his supposed 'effect', that they fail to ensure that their criticisms are founded
even in his biography, let alone his text, and that (in this respect at least resembling their target) they contradict themselves, and each other. I might as well add that I have spoken

on radical platforms with each of the above-mentioned, ex-
cepting only Deutscher (with whose widow, Tamara, I did
once appear), and that though Conor Cruise O'Brien has
long abandoned the Left, he was much prized in his day as a
staunch opponent of both Orwell and — a potentially related author — Albert Camus.

To Edward Thompson one might respond — arcane
though the argument now seems — that if George Orwell
had not mentioned him in about two dozen essays, the very
name of Tom Wintringham might very well have been forgotten. Returned from service with the International Brigade
in Spain, and disillusioned with Stalin's methods, Wintringham — along with Orwell's close friend Humphrey Slater —
proposed that Britain adopt a 'people's war' defence against
the menace of Nazi invasion. Despite many official misgivings, he was given command of the Osterley Park headquarters, and helped popularize the idea of an armed but volun-
tary 'Home Guard'. This military doctrine, designed both to
raise the cost of a German landing and to involve and train
those who were above military age, found its most assiduous
proselytizer in Orwell. His wartime journalism is at times almost obsessed with the topic; he saw in it the hope of a de-
mocratized future Britain as well as the memory of a defeated
republican Spain.

As for James Burnham, the intellectual father of the
Cold War (who belongs in my next chapter), Orwell was one
of the very few commentators to see the sinister influence
of his preachings, and to subject these to a critique which
greatly nettled Burnham himself. Nobody reading Orwell

on Burnham could possibly conclude that he had found any sort of 'confirmation' in him. The case is precisely to the contrary.

Salman Rushdie repeats Thompson's error about quietism (and also his title, though he maintains that this is coincidental) by taking phrases that Orwell puts in the mouth of others, and attributing them to their author. Thus in 'Inside the Whale' Orwell writes: 'Progress and reaction have both turned out to be swindles'; 'Give yourself over to the world-process . . . simply accept it, endure it, record it' will be 'the formula that any sensitive novelist is now likely to adopt'. What could be plainer? It is so evidently not his own view that one does not need the evidence — a desperate last decade of activism and commitment to democracy and decolonization, and the writing of two novels with an urgent anti-totalitarian tone — of his own career in order to refute it. I hesitate to point this out to a dear friend who is a far more vigilant reader than myself, but the fallacy of awarding an author's third-person lines and characters' traits to himself is a blunder one is taught to avoid and abhor at an early age.

I don't know why Edward Said thinks that it is morally important to make lifelong friends of those one encounters when making journalistic or sociological researches, but it is scandalously unfair of him to say that Orwell 'dropped' those he met while he was investigating slum and factory conditions, or while he was fighting in Spain. He kept up, through visits and correspondence, with a number of the first group — notably the 'proletarian' writer Jack Common, for whom he often tried to find work and to whom he lent his cottage.

And his letters and public statements show a lifetime of commitment to those he had known in Spain, or to those of that group who had survived either death at the front or execution by Stalinist police in the rear. He worked to get them out of prison, to publicize their cases, to help their families and — perhaps most important — to save them from obloquy. All of this is to be found in the published record.

Nor have I any idea why Said should consider Orwell's life a 'comfortable' one. Having taken a bullet through the throat, and while suffering from a demoralizing and ultimately lethal case of TB, he lived on an astonishingly low budget and tried whenever possible to grow his own food and even to make his own furniture. Indeed, if there was anything affected about him it might be his indifference to bourgeois life, his almost ostentatious austerity. In the same essay, Said (who is reviewing Peter Stansky and William Abrams, co-authors obsessed with the Blair/Orwell distinction) congratulates them on their forceful use of tautology:

> 'Orwell belonged to the category of writers who write.'
> And could afford to write, they might have added. In contrast they speak of George Garrett, whom Orwell met in Liverpool, a gifted writer, seaman, dockworker, Communist militant, 'the plain facts of [whose] situation — on the dole, married and with kids, the family crowded into two rooms — made it impossible for him to attempt any extended piece of writing.' Orwell's writing life then was from the start an affirmation of unexamined bourgeois values.

This is rather extraordinary. Orwell did indeed meet Garrett in Liverpool in 1936, and was highly impressed to find that he knew him already through his pseudonymous writing — under the name Matt Lowe — for John Middleton Murry's *Adelphi*. As he told his diary:

> I urged him to write his autobiography, but as usual, living in about 2 rooms on the dole with a wife (who I gather objects to his writing) and a number of kids, he finds it impossible to settle to any long work and can only do short stories. Apart from the enormous unemployment in Liverpool it is almost impossible for him to get work because he is blacklisted everywhere as a Communist.

Thus the evidence that supposedly shames Orwell by contrast is in fact supplied by — none other than Orwell himself! This is only slightly better than the other habit of his foes, which is to attack him for things he quotes other people as saying, as if he had instead said them himself. (The idea that a writer must be able to 'afford' to write is somewhat different and, as an idea, is somewhat — to use a vogue term of the New Left — 'problematic'. If it were only the bourgeois who were able to write, much work would never have been penned and, incidentally, Orwell would never have met Garrett in the first place.)

As for the black and brown 'mobs': I hope I have said enough on the subject. Orwell criticized Gandhi at the height of his popularity for relying too much on 'soul-force' and non-violence, and for being too passive in his resistance.

At the liberation of Addis Ababa (capital of what was then Abyssinia and is now Ethiopia) from Italian fascism, he growled at the fact that the Union Jack was raised before the Abyssinian flag. He never let his readers forget that they lived off an empire of overseas exploitation, writing at one point that, try as Hitler might, he could not reduce the German people to the abject status of Indian coolies. And so on, consistently.

Isaac Deutscher was best known — like his compatriot Joseph Conrad — for learning English at a late age and becoming a prose master in it. But when he writes above, about the 'fact' that millions of people 'may' conclude something, he commits a solecism in any language. Like many other critics, he judges Orwell's *Nineteen Eighty-Four* not as a novel or even as a polemic, but by the possibility that it may depress people. This has been the standard by which priests and censors have adjudged books to be lacking in that essential 'uplift' which makes them wholesome enough for mass consumption. The pretentious title of Deutscher's essay only helps to reinforce the impression of something surreptitious being attempted.

Raymond Williams, who introduced two generations of English readers to the idea of 'cultural studies', is my prime offender and I'm saving him up for later. But he also, if you notice, judges a book by its reception. Conor Cruise O'Brien is no longer on the Left but he still likes to argue by employing rhetoric like this, and one is faced with this dilemma: did he read Orwell on Kipling and Empire and decide for some undisclosed reason of his own that the author didn't mean a word of it? Or did he just not read it at all? This question does not lose its force simply because O'Brien himself has made the transition all the way from Red and Green — via a slightly empurpled phase — to flag-waving Orange.

I did not select the above quotations because they were easy meat, and could be made short work of. In all instances, they are the core statements of the authors concerned, and if anything they understate the animus against Orwell which the mainstream Left has always nurtured. But it is not usual to catch such distinguished writers in the act of making such elementary mistakes. Can it be that the animus has been allowed to depose the ordinary intellectual standard? And if so, why?

The condemnation of Aristides the Just, in ancient Athens, is said by some to have occurred because people were irritated by hearing him referred to as 'the Just'. And the plaster-saint element in Orwell's reputation has always irritated his critics. (It would have surprised Orwell, too, if he had survived to see it.) Making allowance for this annoyance, how is one to account for the way that it incites people to self-evident distortions?

To return to my point about the immense *power* that his enemies attribute to him. Orwell once wrote about the 'large, vague renown' that constituted the popular memory of Thomas Carlyle. His own reputation has long been of that kind, if not rather greater and more precise. But this is not the same as moving millions to despair and apathy (Deutscher), or spoiling the morale of a whole generation (Williams), or authoring a work of fiction that was in fact, in rather cunning disguise, the work of an entire 'culture' (Thompson). In some semi-articulated way, many major figures of the Left have thought of Orwell as an *enemy*, and an important and frightening one.

This was true to a somewhat lesser extent in his own lifetime. And, again, the dislike or distrust can be illustrated by a simple — or at any rate a simple-minded — confusion of categories. It was widely said, and believed, of Orwell that he had written the damning sentence: 'The working classes smell.' This statement of combined snobbery and heresy was supposedly to be found in *The Road to Wigan Pier*, in other words — since the book was a main selection of Victor Gollancz's Left Book Club — it could be checked and consulted. But it obviously never was checked or consulted, because in those pages Orwell only says that middle-class people, such as his own immediate forebears, were convinced that the working classes smelled. Victor Gollancz himself, though hopelessly at odds with Orwell in matters of politics, issued a denial on his behalf that he had ever said, or written, that 'the working classes smell'. It made no difference. As his published correspondence shows, every time Orwell wrote anything objectionable to the Left, up would come this old charge again, having attained the mythic status that placed it beyond mere factual refutation. It feels silly even to go over this pettiness again, but the identical method — of attributing to him the outlook that he attributed to others — is employed in our own time in critical discussions of 'Inside the Whale'.

One figure of the Left can be taken as representative of the general hostility. Raymond Williams was a member of the Communist generation of the 1930s and 1940s. (His first published work, co-authored with Eric Hobsbawm, was a Cambridge student pamphlet defending the Soviet Union's invasion of Finland in the period of the Hitler–Stalin pact.) He forsook Communist orthodoxy to become, with E. P. Thompson and Stuart Hall, one of the germinal figures of the 1950s New Left. And when the old New Left fell out with the new New Left (these things do happen), he was one of those who continued to be revered by the younger generation of *Marxisant* and continentalized intellectuals grouped around Perry Anderson at the *New Left Review*. In 1979, indeed, New Left Books published a volume-length series of respectful interviews and conversations with Williams, entitled *Politics and Letters*.

Let me begin where Williams does, in his immensely influential book *Culture and Society*, published in 1958. The first mention of Orwell comes in a discussion of George Gissing:

> If Gissing is less compassionately observant than Mrs Gaskell, less overtly polemical than Kingsley, still *The Nether World* and *Demos* would be sympathetically endorsed by either of them, or by their typical readers. Yet Gissing does introduce an important new element, and one that remains significant. He has often been called 'the spokesman of despair', and this is true in both meanings of the phrase. Like Kingsley and Mrs Gaskell, he writes to describe the true conditions of the poor, and to protest against those brute forces of society which fill with wreck the abysses of

the nether world. Yet he is also the spokesman of another
kind of despair: the despair born of social and political disil-
lusion. In this he is a figure exactly like Orwell in our own
day, and for much the same reason. Whether one calls this
honesty or not will depend on experience.

Orwell later gets a chapter to himself, in which Williams
grandly announces that 'the total effect of [his] work is an effect of paradox. He was a humane man who communicated
an extreme of inhuman terror; a man committed to decency
who actualized a distinctive squalor.'

To the first point one might reply by observing that
Orwell was a tremendous admirer of George Gissing, and
made frequent references to his novels, especially *The Private Papers of Henry Ryecroft*, *The Odd Women*, *Demos* and
New Grub Street. In a sketch of the author published in
1943, he wrote:

> Here was a humane, intelligent man, of scholarly tastes,
> forced into intimacy with the London poor, and his con-
> clusion was simply this: these people are savages who
> must on no account be allowed political power. In a more
> excusable form it is the ordinary reaction of the
> lower-middle-class man who is near enough to the work-
> ing class to be afraid of them. Above all, Gissing grasped
> that the middle class suffer more from economic insecu-
> rity than the working class, and are more ready to take ac-
> tion against it. To ignore that fact has been one of the ma-
> jor blunders of the Left, and from this sensitive novelist

who loved Greek tragedies, hated politics and began writing long before Hitler was born, one can learn something of the origins of Fascism.

Now as it happens, I know for certain that Williams had seen Orwell's early and late work on George Gissing. When he was helping to edit the journal *Politics and Letters* in post-war Cambridge, along with Wolf Mankowitz and Clifford Collins, he was given the manuscript of a longer Gissing essay by Orwell himself, who was by then desperately ill and confined to a Scottish sanatorium. The manuscript was lost and never returned to Orwell; the magazine itself (having been devoted to a rather forbidding fusion of the ideas of Karl Marx and F. R. Leavis) then folded. Williams's own account of this fiasco — the manuscript was found again in 1959 — is quite exceptionally ungenerous. And it doesn't take a literary detective, scanning the passage above, to notice that he is partly saying of Orwell what Orwell actually says about Gissing. This half-buried resentment can be further noticed when Williams turns to paradox. I have already insisted that Orwell contains opposites and even contradictions, but where is the paradox in a 'humane man who communicated an extreme of inhuman terror'? Where is the paradox in 'a man committed to decency who actualized a distinctive squalor'? The choice of verbs is downright odd, if not a little shady. 'Communicated'? 'Actualized'? Assuming that Williams means to refer to *Nineteen Eighty-Four* in the first case, which he certainly does, would it not be more precise to say that Orwell 'evoked' or even 'prefigured' or perhaps simply 'described' an extreme of inhuman terror? Yet that choice of verb, because more accurate, would be less 'paradoxical'. Because what Williams means to imply, but is not brave enough to say, is that Orwell 'invented' the picture of totalitarian collectivism.

As for 'actualizing' a distinctive squalor, the author of that useful book *Keywords* has here chosen a deliberately inexact term. He may mean *Nineteen Eighty-Four* again — he is obsessed with the 'gritty dust' that infests Orwell's opening passage — or he may mean the depictions of the mean and cramped (and malodorous) existence imposed on the denizens of Wigan Pier. But to 'actualize' such squalor is either to make it real — no contradiction to decency — or to make it actually *occur*, a suggestion which is obviously nonsensical.

Later on in *Culture and Society*, Williams scores a few points by reprinting some absolutist sentences that, taken on their own, represent exaggerations or generalizations. It was a strength and weakness of Orwell's polemical journalism that he would begin an essay with a bold and bald statement designed to arrest attention — a tactic that, as Williams rightly notices, he borrowed in part from G. K. Chesterton and George Bernard Shaw. No regular writer can re-read his own output of ephemera without encountering a few wince-making moments of this kind; Williams admits to 'isolating' them but has some fun all the same. The flat sentence 'a humanitarian is always a hypocrite' may contain a particle of truth — does in fact contain such a particle — but will not quite do on its own. Other passages of Orwell's, on the failure of the Western socialist movement, read more convincingly now than they did when Williams was mocking them, but are somewhat sweeping for all that. And there are the famous outbursts of ill-temper against cranks and vegetarians and homosexuals, which do indeed disfigure the prose and (even though we still admire Pope and Swift for the heroic unfairness of their invective) probably deserve rebuke. However, Williams betrays his hidden bias even when addressing these relatively easy targets. He upbraids Orwell for the repeated use of the diminutive word 'little' as an insult ('The typical Socialist . . . a prim little man', 'the typical little bowler-hatted sneak' etc.). Now, it is probable that we all overuse the term 'little' and its analogues. Williams does at one point — rather 'loftily' perhaps — reproach his New Left colleagues for being too ready to dismiss Orwell as 'petit-bourgeois'. But what about (I draw the example at random) Orwell's disgust at the behaviour of the English crowd in the First World War, when 'wretched little German bakers and hairdressers had their shops sacked by the mob'?

Making another effort to be paradoxical, Williams decides to identify Orwell as an instance of 'the paradox of the exile'. This, which he also identified with D. H. Lawrence, constituted an actual 'tradition', which, in England:

> attracts to itself many of the liberal virtues: empiricism, a certain integrity, frankness. It has also, as the normally contingent virtue of exile, certain qualities of perception: in particular, the ability to distinguish inadequacies in the groups which have been rejected. It gives, also, an appearance of strength, although this is largely illusory. The qualities, though salutary, are largely negative; there is an

appearance of hardness (the austere criticism of hypocrisy,
complacency, self-deceit), but this is usually brittle, and at
times hysterical: the substance of community is lacking,
and the tension, in men of high quality, is very great.

This is quite a fine passage, even when Williams is engaged
in giving with one hand and taking away with the other.
Orwell's working title for *Nineteen Eighty-Four* was 'The
Last Man in Europe'; and there are traces of a kind of solip-
sistic nobility elsewhere in his work, the attitude of the
flinty and solitary loner. May he not be valued, however, as
the outstanding English example of the dissident intellectual who preferred above all other allegiances the loyalty to
truth? Self-evidently, Williams does not believe this and the
clue is in the one word, so seemingly innocuous in itself,
'community'.

For Williams, having awarded Orwell the title of exile,
immediately replaces it with the description 'vagrant'. A vagrant will, for example, not be reassured or comforted by
Williams's not-very-consoling insistence that: '"Totalitarian"
describes a certain kind of repressive social control, but, also,
any real society, any adequate community, is necessarily a to-
tality. To belong to a community is to be a part of a whole,
and, necessarily, to accept, while helping to define, its disci-
plines.' In other words, Williams is inviting Orwell and all of
us to step back inside the whale! Remember your roots, observe the customs of the tribe, recognize your responsibili-
ties. The life of the vagrant or exile is unwholesome, even
dangerous or deluded. The warmth of the family and the

people is there for you; so is the life of the 'movement'. If you must criticize, do so from within and make sure that your criticisms are constructive.

This rather peculiar attempt to bring Orwell back into the fold is reinforced by this extraordinary sentence: 'The principle he chose was socialism, and *Homage to Catalonia* is still a moving book (quite apart from the political controversy it involves) because it is a record of the most deliberate attempt he ever made to become part of a believing community.' I leave it to any reader of those pages to find evidence for such a proposition; it is true that Orwell was very moved by the Catalan struggle and by the friends he made in the course of it. But he wasn't exactly deracinated before he went, and the 'believing community' of which, in the aftermath, he formed a part was a community of revolutionary sympathizers who had felt the shared experience of betrayal at the hands of Stalin. And of Stalin's 'community', at that epoch, Williams formed an organic part.

Nor, by the time he wrote *Culture and Society*, had he entirely separated from it. In a very brief and superficial consideration of *Animal Farm* and *Nineteen Eighty-Four*, he once again set himself doggedly to confuse the medium with the message. In *Animal Farm* 'the issue of government lies between drunkards and pigs, and that is as far as things can go. In *Nineteen Eighty-Four*, the same point is clear, and the terms are now direct. The hated politicians are in charge, while the dumb mass of "proles" goes on very much in its own ways, protected by its very stupidity. The only dissent comes from a rebel intellectual: the exile against the whole system.'

To underline and emphasize his own inability to do so much as master the plot (who could read *Animal Farm* as a mere contest between drunkards and pigs?), Williams even quoted the paragraph on the proles that controverted what he had just said, the very same paragraph as it happens that Orwell took from the momentary experience of being cheered up by the indomitable cleaning ladies in the conformist halls and corridors of the BBC:

> If there was hope, it must lie in the proles . . . everywhere stood the same solid unconquerable figure, made monstrous by work and child bearing, toiling from birth to death and still singing. Out of those mighty loins a race of conscious beings must one day come. You were the dead; theirs was the future. But you could share in that future if you kept alive the mind . . .

In his book *The Captive Mind*, written in 1951–2 and published in the West in 1953, the Polish poet and essayist Czesław Miłosz paid Orwell one of the greatest compliments that one writer has ever bestowed upon another. Miłosz had seen the Stalinization of Eastern Europe from the inside, as a cultural official. He wrote, of his fellow-sufferers:

> A few have become acquainted with Orwell's *1984*; because it is both difficult to obtain and dangerous to possess, it is known only to certain members of the Inner Party. Orwell fascinates them through his insight into details they know well, and through his use of Swiftian satire. Such a form of writing is forbidden by the New

Faith because allegory, by nature manifold in meaning, would trespass beyond the prescriptions of socialist realism and the demands of the censor. Even those who know Orwell only by hearsay are amazed that a writer who never lived in Russia should have so keen a perception into its life.

Only one or two years after Orwell's death, in other words, his book about a secret book circulated only within the Inner Party was itself a secret book circulated only within the Inner Party. Of course, Orwell *had* in a way undergone the experience, and in a relatively direct fashion. Little in his brief life was lost on him; there are premonitions of *Nineteen Eighty-Four* even in his memoir of schooldays 'Such, Such Were the Joys'. Experiences in the colonies and the BBC can be seen to have furnished raw materials; so indeed can his reading of Evgeny Zamyatin's *We* and other dystopian literature from the early days of Stalinism. But the transcendent or crystallizing moment undoubtedly occurred in Spain, or at any rate in Catalonia. This was where Orwell suffered the premonitory pangs of a man living under a police regime: a police regime ruling in the name of socialism and the people. For a Westerner, at least, this epiphany was a relatively novel thing; it brushed the sleeves of many thoughtful and humane people, who barely allowed it to interrupt their preoccupation with the 'main enemy', fascism. But on Orwell it made a permanent impression.

Coincidence, said Louis Pasteur, has a tendency to occur only to the mind that is prepared to notice it. He was speaking of the kind of openness of mind that allows elementary

scientific innovation to occur, but the metaphor is a service-
able one. Orwell was, to an extent, conditioned to keep his
eyes open in Spain, and to register the evidence. It is often
said in mitigation of the intellectuals of the 1930s that they
could not really have known what Stalinism was like. It is
also said — sometimes by the same apologists — that when
they *were* able to guess what Stalinism was like, they also
managed to repress their misgivings for the good of the
cause. A striking fact about Orwell, a tribute to his 'power of
facing', is that he never underwent a Stalinoid phase, never
had to be cured or purged by sudden 'disillusionment'. It is
also true that he was somewhat impatient with those who
pleaded their original illusions as excuses for later naiveté.
This — with its potential hint of superiority — is certainly
part of the reason for the intense dislike he aroused then and
arouses still.

In stark and complete contrast to the torpid 'community' loyalty of men like Raymond Williams, the initial critique of Stalinism was made by a movement of dissident
workers and independent intellectuals. That one or two of
these latter were public-school types who had learned to distrust the idea of 'team spirit' need not surprise anybody; the
First World War had already produced a small but vital
group of conscientious junior officers who 'saw through' jingoism and class allegiance in almost precisely the same way,
and by dint of equally bitter experience.

It only remains to be said that in 1953 — three years after Orwell's death — the workers of East Berlin protested
against their new bosses. In 1956 the masses in Budapest
followed suit, and from 1976 until the implosion of the

'people's democracies', the shipyard workers of Poland were the celebrated shock troops who mocked the very idea of a 'workers' party'. This movement of people and nations was accompanied by the efforts and writings of many 'exile' and 'vagrant' intellectuals, from Miłosz himself to Václav Havel, Rudolf Bahro, Miklós Haraszti, Leszek Kołakowski, Milan Šimečka and Adam Michnik. Not one of these failed to pay some tribute to George Orwell. So the alliance — between communities of workers and alienated sceptics — did come to something after all. One is forced to conclude, however, that this was not at all the healthy and progressive revolution that Raymond Williams had in mind. Least of all was it the outcome of despair and resignation. This is why the work of Orwell will be reread and appreciated — I was about to say 'long after Williams has been forgotten' but I forbid myself the cliché and prefer to say — whether Williams is read and remembered or not.

He wrote a great deal about Orwell but, suggestively in my opinion, omitted any but the very briefest mention of his essays on popular culture. ('In the Britain of the fifties,' as Williams sourly told his interviewers at *New Left Review* in 1979, 'along every road that you moved, the figure of Orwell seemed to be waiting. If you tried to develop a new kind of popular cultural analysis, there was Orwell; if you wanted to report on work or ordinary life, there was Orwell'. . . Does this sound like acknowledgement, or like envy?) Orwell was perhaps the first among the intellectuals to show interest in the recreational aspects of mass literacy and the age of mass production. In his landmark essay 'Boys' Weeklies' he not only made some shrewd points about the manipulation of taste by the press barons but also guessed — correctly as it turned out — that the output of 'Frank Richards', creator of Billy Bunter, was too vast and too homogenized to be the work of one man. (The soft porn for the proles, written by semi-automated machinery, in *Nineteen Eighty-Four* owes something to this insight.) His study of vulgar seaside postcards and their relationship to music-hall humour discovered an artist and draughtsman in Donald McGill. He proposed writing a study of women's weekly magazines which he may or may not have produced; it is sad to think of it being lost, possibly when his Islington home was blitzed in 1944. He monitored the rise and fall of the ethnic joke, noticing that its targets fluctuated with political developments and registering the subtle distinction between jests at the expense of Jews and those which were at the expense of Scotsmen. As a cinema critic he developed a sharp eye for the increasing influence of American marketing techniques on British habits and manners, as well as on British culture in general. It would not be too much to say that he pioneered 'cultural studies' without giving the subject a name. (He might have preferred to say that the proper study of mankind is man.) Post-colonial studies owes something to Orwell also, which is why it is depressing, and I hope not significant, to find Edward Said, as well as Raymond Williams, treating him with such an apparent lack of generosity.

There isn't much room for doubt about the real source of anti-Orwell resentment. In the view of many on the official Left, he committed the ultimate sin of 'giving ammunition to the enemy'. Not only did he do this in the 30s, when the cause of anti-fascism supposedly necessitated a closing of ranks, but he repeated the offence in the opening years of the Cold War and thus — 'objectively', as people used to say — became an ally of the forces of conservatism.

Unlike innumerable contemporaries, whose defections from Communism were later to furnish spectacular confessions and memoirs, Orwell never went through a phase of Russophilia or Stalin-worship or fellow-travelling. He wrote in mid 1940 that he had learned to trust his gut on certain questions:

> Since 1934 I have known war between England and Germany was coming, and since 1936 I have known it with complete certainty. I could feel it in my belly, and the chatter of the pacifists on the one hand, and the Popular Front people who pretended to fear that Britain was preparing for war against Russia on the other, never deceived me. Similarly such horrors as the Russian purges never surprised me, because I had always felt that — not *exactly* that, but something *like* that — was implicit in Bolshevik rule.

Are we to believe that Orwell (who confided the above to his private diary) was able on internal literary evidence to decide that Soviet Communism was monstrous? The claim is partly justified by an incisive review he wrote in June 1938, discussing Eugene Lyons's journalistic memoir *Assignment in Utopia*:

To get the full sense of our ignorance as to what is really happening in the U.S.S.R., it is worth trying to translate the most sensational Russian event of the past two years, the Trotskyist trials, into English terms. Make the necessary adjustments, let Left be Right and Right be Left, and you get something like this:

> Mr. Winston Churchill, now in exile in Portugal, is plotting to overthrow the British Empire and establish Communism in England. By the use of unlimited Russian money he has succeeded in building up a huge Churchillite organisation which includes members of Parliament, factory managers, Roman Catholic bishops and practically the whole of the Primrose League. Almost every day some dastardly act of sabotage is laid bare — sometimes a plot to blow up the House of Lords, sometimes an outbreak of foot and mouth disease in the Royal racing-stables. Eighty per cent of the Beefeaters at the Tower are discovered to be agents of the Comintern. A high official at the Post Office admits brazenly to having embezzled postal orders to the tune of £5,000,000, and also to having committed *lèse majesté* by drawing moustaches on postage stamps. Lord Nuffield, after a 7-hour interrogation by Mr. Norman Birkett, confesses that ever since 1920 he has been fomenting strikes in his own factories. Casual half-inch paras in every issue of the newspapers announce that fifty more

Churchillite sheep-stealers have been shot in Westmoreland or that the proprietress of a village shop in the Cotswolds has been transported to Australia for sucking the bullseyes and putting them back in the bottle. And meanwhile the Churchillites (or Churchillite-Harmsworthites as they are called after Lord Rothermere's execution) never cease from proclaiming that it is *they* who are the real defenders of Capitalism and that Chamberlain and the rest of his gang are no more than a set of Bolsheviks in disguise.

Anyone who has followed the Russian trials knows that this is scarcely a parody . . . From our point of view the whole thing is not merely incredible as a genuine conspiracy, it is next door to incredible as a frame-up. It is simply a dark mystery, of which the only seizable fact — sinister enough in its way — is that Communists over here regard it as a good advertisement for Communism.

Meanwhile the truth about Stalin's régime, if we could only get hold of it, is of the first importance. Is it Socialism, or is a particularly vicious form of state-capitalism?

Orwell answered the question with a verdict in favour of the latter. His essay is worth citing at length because it shows, first, that he was capable of writing humorously (a vein in which he did not allow himself much exercise), and second, that he could make a large and intelligent inference from very limited information. It was not only committed Communists who took the fantastic confessions of the Moscow defendants at face value. Eminent jurists and QCs, veteran reporters and parliamentarians, ministers of religion, all found that the sheer volume of evidence was impressive and convincing. Writing for the small audience of the *New English Weekly*, Orwell backed his instinct about the hideous language of the process, as well as its hysterical irrationality, and pronounced it a gigantic fraud.

He was not relying entirely on instinct. In Spain, he had seen Stalinist frame-ups and falsified denunciations at first hand, and come closer than he ever knew to having been a victim of them. Moreover, as the telling phrase 'state-capitalism' shows us, he was in contact with the small and scattered forces of the independent international Left — forces now largely forgotten, but containing important individuals who witnessed at a critical time, and at immense risk, to the menace of totalitarianism.

The generic name for this movement was Trotskyist ('Trotskyite' or 'Trotsky-Fascist' as the Moscow line put it). Orwell never called himself a follower of Leon Trotsky, though he did base the figure of Emmanuel Goldstein, reviled heretic of *Nineteen Eighty-Four*, on him and he did say this, about his own Home-Guardist and radical activities during the Second World War: 'England is in some ways politically backward, extremist slogans are not bandied to and fro as they are in continental countries, but the feeling of all true patriots and all true Socialists is at bottom reducible to the "Trotskyist" slogan: "The war and the revolution are inseparable."' This must be the most English form in which cosmopolitan and subversive Trotskyism has ever been cast; Orwell's attempt to connect the leader of the Petrograd Soviet to the stalwarts of 'Dad's Army' is nearly, but not quite, risible. Not quite risible because there was in fact a social and anti-colonial revolution in parallel with the war; an admittedly slow-motion revolution in which Orwell bore an honourable part. And not quite risible because the edifice of his work, so much identified with sturdy English virtues, owes a great deal to the unspoken International of persecuted oppositionists who withstood 'the midnight of the century' — the clasping of hands between Hitler and Stalin.

In Orwell's letters and journalism one finds knowing and educated references to Victor Serge, one of the first to experience the Russian revolution at first hand and then to see in which direction it was tending; to C. L. R. James, the Trinidadian literary genius who wrote *Black Jacobins*, a history of Toussaint L'Ouverture's revolution in Haiti, then quarrelled memorably with the Comintern, and wrote the best book ever published on the ethics and history of cricket; to Boris Souvarine, early historian of anti-Stalinism; and to Panaït Istrati, a prescient analyst of Soviet cultural thuggery. (Istrati wrote the introduction to the French edition of *Down and Out in Paris and London* just before his death in 1935 — the title, *La Vache enrageé*, would now read rather oddly and resonantly to those familiar with the menace of the mad cow; it derives from the Parisian idiom *manger de la vache enragée*, meaning to 'rough it'. It had also been the title of a satirical journal in an earlier Paris, for which Toulouse-Lautrec himself supplied a poster.)

There may be a sort of literary-political alchemy or chemistry which ensures that the right critic notices the right

book, or that the right intellectuals and hard cases come into
contact with one another: Orwell was quick to register the
impact of André Gide's *Retour de l'URSS*, one of the earliest
works by an author who had set out to praise the Moscow
regime and returned in disgust. The editors of *Partisan Review*, a brilliant mixed bag of freelance New York intellectuals broad enough to include Dwight Macdonald and Philip
Rahv, had already decided to fuse their anti-Stalinist politics
with their commitment to literary modernism when they began to cast about for a transatlantic contributor. Their first
choice was Orwell, who composed a regular *London Letter*
between the time of the Munich Agreement and the end of
the war. Desperately ill in the last years of his life, he became
aware of the work of David Rousset, a French dissident leftist whose book *L'Univers Concentrationnaire* was the first literary attempt to establish the 'camp', with all its horrific associations, as a central metaphor in the moral catastrophes of
the century. It was proposed that Rousset might write the
foreword to the French edition of either *Homage to Catalonia* or *Animal Farm*; Orwell had at one point hoped that André Malraux might contribute the former but became
markedly less enthusiastic when he learned of Malraux's support for de Gaulle's regime.

On practical or immediate questions the same essential
clarity is to be found. Orwell took it for granted that there
had been a hideous famine in the Ukraine in the 1930s,
something that was denied by many fellow-travelling journalists who claimed to have visited the scene. In 1940 — a
bad year — he wrote this, about the Poles:

Amid a spate of books about Czechoslovakia and Spain there have not been many about Poland, and this book raises once again the painful question of small nationalities. As it happens I recently saw it reviewed in a left-wing paper under the heading 'Fascist Poland did not deserve to survive.' The implication was that the state of independent Poland was so bad that the downright slavery instituted by Hitler was preferable. Ideas of this kind were undoubtedly gaining ground between the outbreak of war and June, 1940. In the Popular Front period left-wing opinion was committed to defending the crazy pavement of Versailles, but the Russo-German pact upset the 'antifascist' orthodoxy of the past few years. It became the fashion to say that small nationalities were a nuisance and that Poland was 'just as bad as' Nazi Germany . . . But actually the Polish army fought as long as the French, against far heavier odds, nor did the Poles suddenly change sides in the middle of the war. It seems, in fact, that this nation of thirty million souls, with its long tradition of struggle against the Emperor and the Tsar, deserves its independence in any world where national sovereignty is possible. Like the Czechs, the Poles will rise again, though the old feudal life, with the private chapel in the castle grounds and the gamekeeper who is the baron's foster-brother, is vanished for ever.

One may notice that Orwell employs the term 'souls', somewhat uncharacteristic of him, but also that he remembers, as he usually did, to avoid the romanticization of the victims. A few months before this *New Statesman* essay was written, W. H. Auden (a poet he had criticized unfairly) had written 'September 1, 1939'. In that numinous poem, Auden spoke of the whole civilized world lying 'defenceless under the night':

> *Yet, dotted everywhere,*
> *Ironic points of light*
> *Flash out wherever the Just*
> *Exchange their messages:*

In some fashion, Orwell's signals were picked up and returned by those in a position to receive and then retransmit them. It was a signal of that sort that was heard by Czesław Miłosz in Poland many years later, even when its original transmitter had gone dead.

The nearest that Orwell came to anything that might be termed Trotskyism was in Spain, where he went to the Lenin barracks in Barcelona and enlisted in the militia of the POUM (Workers' Party of Marxist Unification or *Partido Obrero de Unificación Marxista*, a party which, while not itself 'Trotskyist', had a sympathetic attitude to the Left Opposition). But he took this step because of a relatively happy accident — that of his prior association with the distinctly home-grown Independent Labour Party (ILP) which, critical of the Labour Party from the Left, took an anti-Stalinist position also. (Its most distinguished member was Fenner Brockway, later a leading Labour parliamentarian and renowned champion of colonial independence.) Most foreign anti-fascists either enlisted in, or were selected for, the

International Brigades, which operated under strict Communist Party discipline. Orwell's signing up with a dissident band allowed him to see at first hand the real story in Catalonia, which was the story of a revolution betrayed.

This is not the place to tell the entire tale. But most chroniclers and historians are now in agreement: Orwell told the truth, in his *Homage to Catalonia*, about the deliberate subversion of the Spanish Republic by the agents of Stalin, and about the especially ruthless way in which they tried to destroy Catalonia's independent Left. As it happens, he was an eyewitness of the attempted Communist coup in Barcelona in early May 1937, and newly available documents from the Soviet Military Archive in Moscow make it plain that a full-scale putsch was in fact intended. Had it succeeded, then plans for another 'show trial', along the lines of the Moscow frame-ups, were in train. Even as it was, the great Catalan leader Andrés Nin, founder of the POUM, was kidnapped, savagely tortured and — on refusing to crack — murdered. It was then said by Communist spokesmen that he had fled to join the Nazis.

Orwell never knew it, but had he and his wife not managed to escape from Spain with the police at their heels they might well have been placed in the dock as exhibits for that very show trial. A memorandum from the archives of the KGB (then known as the NKVD), dated 13 July 1937, describes him and Eileen O'Shaughnessy as 'pronounced Trotskyites' operating with clandestine credentials. It also asserts, with the usual tinge of surreal fantasy, that the couple maintained contact with opposition circles in Moscow. This

accusation would have been no joke in the hands of an inter-
rogator, even though Orwell makes the least of it in *Homage
to Catalonia*. 'I was not guilty of any definite act,' he wrote,
'but I was guilty of "Trotskyism". The fact that I had served
with the POUM militia was quite enough to get me into
prison.' More than enough, in fact, if the individual concerned had made himself or herself conspicuous. Orwell re-
counts in a slightly farcical and self-deprecating tone the
seizure of papers and letters from his wife's hotel room, but
these documents, he might have been surprised to learn, were
later scrutinized by Moscow. Friends of Orwell's, like his
brigade commander George Kopp, were imprisoned under
the foulest conditions and — in Kopp's case, prefiguring the
horrific climax of *Nineteen Eighty-Four* — subjected to
the torture of close confinement with rats. Others, like the
brave working-class volunteer Bob Smillie, died of the treatment they received.*

'All I have is a voice/,' wrote Auden in that same poem
'September 1, 1939', 'to undo the folded lie,/The romantic
lie in the brain/Of the sensual man-in-the-street/And the lie
of Authority/.' Orwell had barely even a voice when he left
Catalonia; a fascist bullet had torn through his throat and
damaged his vocal chords. But for the next ten years of his
life, which were also the last, he wrote to try and vindicate
his Spanish friends and their cause. It suited Authority in the
West, and some of the men-in-the-street too, to maintain

---

*For a fuller account of the revelations of the Moscow archives, and their detailed
vindication of Orwell, see my Introduction to *Orwell in Spain* (Penguin, 2001).

that the war was what it seemed — Catholic nationalist Spain on one side and 'Red' anti-clerical Spain on the other. (It also suited Stalin's supporters to be taken at their own valuation.) Orwell was thus in a unique and challenging position for a writer; he knew that the whole picture was false and the whole story was a lie, and he had only his own integrity as a soldier and a writer to back him up. His despatches from Spain were almost unpublishable — the *New Statesman* famously refused to print them because they might let down the republican side — and *Homage to Catalonia* was an obscure collector's item of a book throughout Orwell's lifetime. More important to him than these difficulties was this impressive and intimidating thought:

> It will never be possible to get a completely accurate and unbiased account of the Barcelona fighting, because the necessary records do not exist. Future historians will have nothing to go upon except a mass of accusations and party propaganda. I myself have little data beyond what I saw with my own eyes and what I have learned from other eye-witnesses whom I believe to be reliable . . .
>
> This kind of thing is frightening to me, because it often gives me the feeling that the very concept of objective truth is fading out of the world. After all, the chances are that those lies, or at any rate similar lies, will pass into history . . . The implied objective of this line of thought is a nightmare world in which the Leader, or some ruling clique, controls not only the future but *the past*. If the Leader says of such and such an event, 'It never happened'

— well, it never happened. If he says that two and two are
five — well, two and two are five.

Here again we can feel the lengthening shadow of *Nineteen
Eighty-Four*. And in some ways, Orwell's prediction was ful-
filled. The lie did become accepted, for a while. In 1971, in
the prestige series 'Modern Masters', which enjoyed a great
publishing vogue, none other than Raymond Williams was
invited to summarize the significance of Orwell for a new
generation. And there was no protest when he wrote, of
Homage to Catalonia, that:

> Most historians have taken the view that the revolution
> — mainly anarcho-syndicalist but with the POUM tak-
> ing part — was an irrelevant distraction from a desperate
> war. Some, at the time and after, have gone so far as to de-
> scribe it as deliberate sabotage of the war effort. Only a
> few have argued on the other side, that the suppression of
> the revolution by the main body of Republican forces was
> an act of power politics, related to Soviet policy, which
> amounted to a betrayal of the cause for which the Spanish
> people were fighting.

This short drab paragraph manages to be replete with ingen-
ious dishonesty and evasion. The words 'most historians' are
meaningless; no such consensus exists or ever has. We are not
told which 'historians' take the view that Nin and Orwell were
'deliberate' saboteurs; in other words that they were fascists or
fascist sympathizers. The third possible view, attributed
to 'only a few', is stated with the maximum of euphemism.

'Suppression' is a much nicer term than murder or torture or rigged trial. 'The main body of Republican forces' sounds good, if deliberately vague. 'Power politics' is a neutral way of saying realpolitik; it gives an impression of stern but regrettable necessity. And what is one to say of 'related to Soviet policy'? A minor masterpiece of understatement, intended to obscure even the thought of Stalin and his death squads. Of the May 1937 killings in Barcelona, Williams writes two pages later that they took place 'in the name of the struggle against fascism, and, most accounts say, in the name of the true cause of socialism and of the people'. Again there is the surreptitious and gutless reliance on the non-existent 'most accounts'. This is the sort of bureaucratese, combined with intellectual corruption, of which Orwell had written, in 'Politics and the English Language' in 1945: 'Political language — and with variations this is true of all political parties, from Conservatives to Anarchists — is designed to make lies sound truthful and murder respectable, and to give an appearance of solidity to pure wind.'

In his writing on *Nineteen Eighty-Four*, Williams was even worse. As he phrased it with almost deliberate obtuseness:

> It needs to be said, however bitterly, that if the tyranny of *1984* ever finally comes, one of the major elements of the ideological preparation will have been just this way of seeing 'the masses', 'the human beings passing you on the pavement', the eighty-five per cent who are *proles*.

Not content with assigning the views of Winston Smith to his creator — one trembles for Williams's students at Cambridge

if they were not taught to avoid this first-year howler —
Williams also indicts Orwell for, as it were, recommending
the course of self-abnegation and betrayal that Smith takes
when he is finally broken, and betrays Julia, in Room 101.
As Williams sees the matter:

> *Under the spreading chestnut tree*
> *I sold you and you sold me.*

> He [Orwell] can describe this accurately as 'a peculiar,
> cracked, braying, jeering note . . . a yellow note', but still
> *it is what he makes happen.* The cynical jingle of the
> rat-race, which in similar forms we have been hearing ever
> since from the agency offices and parties, leads straight to
> the nightmare of the rat in Room 101. Of course people
> break down under torture, but not all people break down
> [my italics].

One reels back. Orwell *makes this happen?* The rat in Room
101 is a rodent produced by the *consumer* society? And beyond this resentful sub-literate attitude is lurking something
worse: of course people *do* break down under torture, otherwise Stalin's trials in Moscow in the 1930s, and in Prague
and Budapest and Sofia in the 1940s, would not have been
possible (and their 'evidence' would not have been swallowed
by intellectuals like Williams). And yes, to be sure, not all
people break down; Andrés Nin was unbreakable and thus
the Stalin trials in Spain did not take place or, where they
were attempted, were contemptible failures. But who has the

right to make this high-minded observation? George Orwell, who steadily opposed such methods, or Raymond Williams, the overrated doyen of cultural studies and Cambridge English, who never uttered a straightforward word about them?

Interviewing Williams on bended knee in 1979, the editors of *New Left Review* smugly asserted that '*Nineteen Eighty-Four* will be a curio in 1984'. In closing, I should like to offer three practical, rather than argumentative, rebuttals to that view; three arguments, if you like, from experience.

In the closing months of the twentieth century, I contrived to get a visa for North Korea. Often referred to as 'the world's last Stalinist state', it might as easily be described as the world's prototype Stalinist state. Founded under the protection of Stalin and Mao, and made even more hermetic and insular by the fact of a partitioned peninsula that so to speak 'locked it in', the Democratic People's Republic of Korea still boasted the following features at the end of the year 2000. On every public building, a huge picture of 'The Great Leader' Kim Il Sung, the dead man who still holds the office of President in what one might therefore term a necrocracy or mausolocracy. (All other senior posts are occupied by his son, 'The Dear Leader' Kim Jong Il — 'Big Brother' was a perversion of family values as well.) Children marched to school in formation, singing songs in praise of aforesaid Leader. Photographs of the Leader displayed by order in every home. A lapel-button, with the features of the Leader, compulsory wear for all citizens. Loudspeakers and radios blasting continuous propaganda for the Leader and the Party. A society endlessly mobilized for war, its propaganda both hysterical and

— in reference to foreigners and foreign powers — intensely chauvinistic and xenophobic. Complete prohibition of any news from outside or any contact with other countries. Absolute insistence, in all books and in all publications, on a unanimous view of a grim past, a struggling present, and a radiant future. Repeated bulletins of absolutely false news of successful missile tests and magnificent production targets. A pervasive atmosphere of scarcity and hunger, alleviated only by the most abysmal and limited food. Grandiose and oppressive architecture. A continuous stress on mass sports and mass exercise. Apparently total repression of all matters connected to the libido. Newspapers with no news, shops with no goods, an airport with almost no planes. A vast nexus of tunnels underneath the capital city, connecting different Party and police and military bunkers.

There was, of course, only one word for it, and it was employed by all journalists, all diplomats and all overseas visitors. It's the only time in my writing life when I have become tired of the term 'Orwellian'. In some respects, the North Korean nightmare falls short of his dystopia: the regime is too poor and too inefficient to provide telescreens or even wireless sets to most of its subjects. In some respects, however, it is infinitely more forbidding: Winston and Julia would have had no chance at all for a moment of private delight in the countryside, let alone the lease of a crummy flat in some anonymous quarter of town. None the less, there really are 'hate' sessions during breaks in factory or office work, and at an evening of 'mass games' I was shown, via multiple hypnotizing flashcards, the hideous image of a grim-visaged 'enemy' soldier hurtling towards me, to be replaced by the refulgent and reassuring face of The Great Leader. These are details; what was entirely unmistakeable was the atmosphere of a society where individual life is *absolutely pointless*, and where everything that is not absolutely compulsory is absolutely forbidden. The resulting dankness and dinginess and misery would have been almost indescribable without reference to a certain short novel that had been bashed out on an old typewriter, against the clock, by a dying English radical half a century before.

There have never been any reported dissidents in North Korea — a few defectors of course, as even The Party in *Nineteen Eighty-Four* was quite ready to admit, the better to arrange hunts for traitors — and we know as yet almost nothing of its secret prisons and remote detention camps. But one prediction I make is that before this book of mine goes on to the remainder shelf we will have found out. Another prediction I make with confidence is that there will turn out to have been individual Koreans who always kept a scrap of culture alive. And the final prediction is the easiest: there will be a new Korean edition of *Nineteen Eighty-Four*.

My second anecdote is both bitter and sweet. Ever since the white-settler revolt in Southern Rhodesia in 1965, I had involved myself with the white and black advocates of majority rule and independence. I made several visits to the country, and interviewed many of the guerrilla leaders in exile, of whom the most impressive was Robert Mugabe. His ultimate election victory in 1980, transforming Rhodesia into Zimbabwe, was a foretaste of the later triumph of Nelson Mandela.

But the abolition of racism and the end of colonial rule was succeeded by a dirty war in Matabeleland against the supporters of Mugabe's rival Joshua Nkomo, and by the awarding of confiscated agricultural property to the party loyalists of the regime. Displaying signs of megalomania, especially after the tragic death of his wife, Mr Mugabe set up a 'youth brigade' that was named the 21st February Movement in honour of his own birthday. He invited North Korean 'advisors' to train his army. And he employed death-squad tactics against the democratic opposition, which based itself on Zimbabwe's trade union movement.

Thus, when the oppositional *Daily News* began to serialize *Animal Farm* in June of 2001 nobody needed to have the joke explained to them. Napoleon, the scheming and ruthless pig who makes his own birthday a holiday and reserves all the milk and beer for his fellow porcines, was depicted in the paper in the heavily rimmed black spectacles worn by Mr Mugabe. Geoffrey Nyarota, the paper's editor-in-chief, remarked that: '*Animal Farm* is not only relevant but pertinent to Zimbabwe. The animals in the book won independence by working together. But in due course some became drunk with power.' Bookshops in the capital city, Harare, could not keep pace with demand for Orwell's classic, which increased when the presses of the *Daily News* were destroyed by an anti-tank mine of the sort not available to ordinary civilians.

My third vignette is briefer and more agreeable. In 1998, near the Barcelona waterfront, a rather plebeian square was named 'Plaça George Orwell' at a ceremony commissioned by the city's socialist mayor, Pasqual Maragall. At around the same time, in the Catalan town of Can Rull, a street was named for Andrés Nin, founder of the POUM. (In this case the presiding official was a member of the Communist Party.) Belated recognition in the first case; belated atonement, perhaps, in the second. But in these understated occasions, with their absence of drilled marching bands, organized salutes and small but unpleasantly noisy orators on large and imposing platforms, one can take a certain comfort that is more than antiquarian. Catalonia has freed itself from the fascism against which Orwell fought, and to which it never submitted. (In the Franco years, even the Catalan language was banned.) It has done so by means of a long and dignified struggle, and it has replaced it by a democratic and pluralist system with a strong radical and leftist flavour. Perhaps most important, however, it has rescued its history and its records from years of falsification and denial. Not even the Catalan Communists now pretend to believe in the lies of the past. Andrés Nin, revered in Catalonia as a great revolutionary and — he might well have disliked the term — martyr, is also available to Catalan schoolchildren and students as the translator of *Anna Karenina* and *Crime and Punishment* into their once-forbidden tongue. How apt that a truly cultured Marxist, tortured and murdered on Stalin's orders, should have upheld Russian literature against the philistinism of Stalin as well as having inspired one of his greatest posthumous defeats.

A triumph for the integrity of history and language, for the cause of the workers and oppressed peoples as well as for the free-thinking intellectual, Catalonia's homage to George

Orwell is more than one had the right to expect. That small, informal investiture and naming in Barcelona summarized much of the moral grandeur of the Left. Marxism in the twentieth century did produce its Andrés Nins as well as its Kim Il Sungs. It's something more than an irony that so many calling themselves leftists have been either too stupid or too compromised to recognize this, or have actually been twisted enough to prefer the second example to the first.

3

Orwell and the Right

Seven wealthy towns contend for Homer dead,
Through which the living Homer begged his bread . . .
✍ THOMAS SEWARD

The attitude of conservative intellectuals and critics towards Orwell's life and work has been a fluctuating and uneven one; it's none the less correct to say that a number of attempts have been made to 'use' him and even to annex him altogether. This is a compliment of a kind, though it can never hope to rise to the unaffected grace of Catalonia's tribute.

It is true on the face of it that Orwell was one of the founding fathers of anti-Communism; that he had a strong patriotic sense and a very potent instinct for what we might call elementary right and wrong; that he despised government and bureaucracy and was a stout individualist; that he distrusted intellectuals and academics and reposed a faith in popular wisdom; that he upheld a somewhat traditional

orthodoxy in sexual and moral matters, looked down on homosexuals and abhorred abortion; and that he seems to have
been an advocate for private ownership of guns. He also preferred the country to the town, and poems that rhymed.

From these scattered bones one could fairly readily (if a
trifle hastily) reconstruct the skeleton of a rather gruff English Home Counties Tory. The mere fact that Orwell spent
his entire adult life in conscious repudiation of this fate and
this identity can be set down to poor upbringing or perhaps
a natural cussedness. Essential soundness will — and did —
emerge in the end. A lifetime of self-education in the opposite direction is of scant interest.

I caricature — I hope — only slightly. There is, fairly certainly, a divided realization in Orwell's writing that the two
things he most valued, which is to say liberty and equality,
were not natural allies of each other. 'A society of free and
equal human beings' — probably his most oft-repeated statement of his preferred objective — seemed unlikely to emerge
from a laissez-faire culture, let alone a laissez-faire culture superimposed, as was the Britain of his time, upon a colonial
and dirigiste one. However, the measures of planning and
taxation and regulation required to make the transition could
easily and obviously eventuate in an over-mighty state with
big ideas of its own. There's not much new in this contradiction; Orwell just happened to register it very acutely. This is
why he admired the spontaneous *fraternity* — the other term
in the 1789 triad — of the Spanish and Catalan republican
forces. It's also why he placed great hope in the native wisdom
and decency of the British, or better say the English, whose

qualities he thought might resolve the problem without too much practical or theoretical difficulty. (This in turn is yet another reason why he is often despised on the Left, which abominates, or at any rate used to abominate, the simple-mindedness of English empiricism.)

The clearest exposition of this divided realization is contained in Orwell's review of *The Road to Serfdom*, by Friedrich August von Hayek. When this short book was first published in 1944, not many people could have appreciated the influence that it was to enjoy. Hayek, a political economist of the Austrian school, had settled in England, and was by a later irony to succeed George Orwell's old foe Harold Laski in the chair at the London School of Economics. His advice to the Conservative Party in the 1945 General Election was widely thought to have been calamitous, in that it encouraged Winston Churchill to make a hugely incautious speech warning that Labour's welfarist plans would require a form of 'Gestapo' to enforce them. That was out of tune with the spirit of the times, and the British Tories were to remain nervously social-democratic until the late 1970s, when Margaret Thatcher broke the political consensus. Among her chosen advisors and mentors was Hayek, who has been of incalculable influence in the revival of free-market theory in Europe and America. (I remember the surprise I felt when hearing him praised by the Yugoslav dissident Milovan Djilas in Belgrade in 1977.)

Orwell's review of *The Road to Serfdom*, which appeared in the *Observer*, could almost have been the crib from which Churchill derived his later speech:

Shortly, Professor Hayek's thesis is that Socialism inevitably leads to despotism, and that in Germany the
Nazis were able to succeed because the Socialists had already done most of their work for them: especially the intellectual work of weakening the desire for liberty. By
bringing the whole of life under the control of the State,
Socialism necessarily gives power to an inner ring of bureaucrats, who in almost every case will be men who want
power for its own sake and will stick at nothing in order
to retain it. Britain, he says, is now going the same road as
Germany, with the Left-Wing intelligentsia in the van
and the Tory Party a good second. The only salvation lies
in returning to an unplanned economy, free competition,
and emphasis on liberty rather than on security.

   In the negative part of Professor Hayek's thesis there
is a great deal of truth. It cannot be said too often — at
any rate, it is not being said nearly often enough — that
collectivism is not inherently democratic, but, on the
contrary, gives to a tyrannical minority such powers as the
Spanish Inquisitors never dreamed of.

(I pause here to note the way in which Orwell, in that last
sentence, managed to step aside and dodge the impact of an
oncoming cliché.) He went on to make some clear objections to Hayek, about the relationship between free competition and monopoly, and the preference of the majority for
even 'State regimentation' over slumps and unemployment,
but it's obvious from several other essays of this period that
the connection between collectivism and despotism was al-

ways worrying some part of his mind. His favourite socialist politician was the great Aneurin Bevan, his editor at *Tribune* and a man of wide culture, who abominated all forms of authoritarianism and, even while fighting the entrenched medical lobbies in his effort to create the National Health Service, once remarked that the socialist movement was the only movement in human history that sought to attain power in order to give it away. For Orwell, there was always the hope that socialists could be for freedom, even if socialism itself had bureaucratic and authoritarian tendencies.

His honesty about this paradox or contradiction is what determined him to write *Nineteen Eighty-Four* as an admonitory parable or fantasy in which 'Ingsoc' — English Socialism — was the Newspeak term for the ruling ideology. It would have been perfectly easy for him to have avoided this crux. In the late 1940s, a dystopian novel based on the notorious horrors of 'National Socialism' would probably have been very well-received. But it would have done nothing to shake the complacency of Western intellectuals concerning the system of state terror for which, at the time, so many of them had either a blind spot or a soft spot.

At best, the Conservative revisionist can claim a small percentage of Orwellian ancestry when it comes to matters of political economy. The point most often reiterated in his writing is that there should be no utilitarian trade-off between *freedom* and *security*. (It might be noticed, in his words on Hayek, that he mentions this Faustian bargain as something with a strong appeal to the masses, rather than to himself.) But he was writing in that almost forgotten time when

Keynes was considered a mere liberal, and when many Tories suspected that laissez-faire was gone for good. Even then, he was a libertarian before the idea had gained currency.

The Conservative reader is entitled to say that, by reviewing Hayek's non-fiction and then composing fiction of his own, Orwell had made the necessary intellectual defection from the Left. But we have his own quite deliberate and considered denial of this interpretation. He issued a number of statements, the most unambivalent of which was sent to Francis Henson of the United Automobile Workers Union. Henson had visited Orwell in 1946 to tell him of the work of a new 'International Rescue and Relief Committee', and Orwell was stirred enough to write to Arthur Koestler to recommend it. Its purpose was:

> to assist victims of totalitarianism, particularly in such matters as giving relief to destitute people, helping political refugees to get out of totalitarian territory, etc. He impressed upon me that this is very definitely a non-Stalinist organisation, that they know all about the Stalinists' ways and are keeping them out of it, and that the organisation is anti-Stalinist to the extent that the people they assist are largely Trotskyists etc.

He appended, among other possible contacts for this work, the address of Victor Serge in Mexico.

Three years later, after that least literary of newspapers the New York *Daily News* had printed an editorial saying that *Nineteen Eighty-Four* was an attack on the British

Labour Government, Orwell was asked by Francis Henson to make a statement and wrote:

> My recent novel is *not* intended as an attack on socialism or on the British Labour Party (of which I am a supporter) but as a show-up of the perversions to which a centralized economy is liable and which have already been partly realized in Communism and fascism . . . The scene of the book is laid in Britain in order to emphasize that the English-speaking races are not innately better than anyone else and that totalitarianism, *if not fought against*, could triumph anywhere.

The Labour government had, after all, just negotiated a fairly honourable independence for India and Burma, an achievement for which socialists had been pressing for some time (and which might have been better accomplished to a socialist timetable than to the expiring rhythms of imperial exhaustion, with its disfiguring accompaniments of scuttle and partition). Notwithstanding this elaborate disavowal or *démenti*, authors in need of a quick fix continued to use even the clapped-out Labourism of the late 1970s as a template for sub-Orwellian literary enterprises. Anthony Burgess's *1985*, published in 1978, had, instead of Airstrip One, a country named 'Tucland', for the old dinosaurs and carthorses of the Trades Union Congress (TUC). In this dystopia, all hotels are run by Arabs, so we have the Al-Dorchester plus, I regret to say, the Al-Idayinn; feral predator gangs are called 'Kumina', the Swahili word for 'teenager'; the population communicates in yob-speak. Even Robert Conquest wrote a poem entitled '1974: Ten Years to Go', in which the menacing figures of Tony Benn, the TUC (again), student Sparts and the IRA were pressed into service. Not all that frightening even at the time, they seem almost quaint today. There is an aesthetic as well as an ideological difference between a deindustrialized banana republic and a hermetic terror state; Orwell's insistence on the distinction was just and necessary.

It is superfluous for Conservatives to claim Orwell as an ally in the Cold War. He was fighting it when most Tories were still hailing Britain's gallant Soviet ally. Indeed, he is credited with coining the term 'cold war', in a paragraph that deserves quotation. On 19 October 1945, in an essay entitled 'You and the Atom Bomb', he drew attention to both the military and the political dangers inherent in a weapon that, not merely unprecedentedly destructive of the innocent, could also only be wielded by an elite:

> We may be heading not for general breakdown but for an
> epoch as horribly stable as the slave empires of antiquity.
> James Burnham's theory has been much discussed, but
> few people have yet considered its ideological implica-
> tions — that is, the kind of world-view, the kind of be-
> liefs, and the social structure that would probably prevail
> in a State which was at once *unconquerable* and in a per-
> manent state of 'cold war' with its neighbours.

It can be seen even from this fragment that Orwell did not conceive of the Cold War as a one-dimensional fight against the totalitarian menace, but as a contest (rather too well-matched) between superpowers, in which the danger of annihilation could be used to petrify and immobilize dissent. He made the same point in more detail on 13 December 1946:

(i) The Russians, whatever they may say, will not agree to genuine inspection of their territories by foreign observers.

(ii) The Americans, whatever they may say, will not let slip the technological lead in armaments.

(iii) No country is now in a condition to fight an all-out major war.

By making the seldom observed distinction (between the Cold War and the arms race or, if you prefer, between the Staliniza-tion of Eastern Europe and the global ambitions of the United States) Orwell took up and separated two threads that were to become fatally entangled in many minds. He could feel the onset of the permanent war economy, and he already knew the use to which permanent war propaganda could be put. This, of course, is why the hideous world of *Nineteen Eighty-Four* is made possible by a constant, shifting hostility between three regional superpowers. (It is also made possible — in a detail that is seldom emphasized — by taking place in a country which has already suffered a limited nuclear 'ex-change', to borrow a cretinous modern euphemism which Or-well would have despised.) When Nixon and Kissinger went to China, which they had more than once threatened with nu-clear attack, and proclaimed that Washington and Beijing were henceforth allies against the Soviet empire, I had already read the news by virtue of studying the abrupt shifts of allegiance between Oceania, Eurasia and Eastasia.

Orwell did more than invent the expression 'cold war'. He was in one sense an early Cold Warrior. Throughout the 1940s, there had been an official conspiracy of silence about the fate of some 10,000 Polish officers, murdered in the forests near Katyn by shots in the back of the neck individually administered by agents of the Soviet secret police. It was not thought politic to mention this atrocity even when well-attested reports came to light. The invading German army, which later uncovered the crime, was instead blamed for committing it (and indeed charged with the responsibility by Soviet lawyers at Nuremberg). Orwell, together with Arthur Koestler and a handful of others, sought to ventilate the matter during the war and afterwards, but were met with official indifference to, and indeed high-level government collusion in, the Soviet lie. The moral atmosphere surrounding the incident is very well captured by Anthony Powell in his novel *The Military Philosophers*, part of the wartime trilogy of his 'Dance to the Music of Time' sequence. The British authorities, Labour and Tory, declined to acknowledge the Soviets' guilt in the matter until July 1988, for fear of 'heating up the Cold War'. The Russian Federation officially accepted responsibility in 1990 . . .

But the essential difference between Orwell and the evolution of the Cold War as a Western political orthodoxy can easily be illustrated by means of his marked disagreement with three leading anti-Communists: T. S. Eliot, James Burnham and — at a posthumous remove — Norman Podhoretz.

I personally cannot read the Orwell–Eliot correspondence without experiencing a deep feeling of contempt. On one side — Orwell's — it consists of a series of friendly and generous invitations: that Eliot should broadcast to India, or read his own work to an Indian audience; that he should join Orwell for lunch in the Fitzroy neighbourhood; that he should come to dinner at Orwell's new family home and (if blitz conditions made this preferable) stay the night there as well. On Eliot's side, all I can locate are some formal costive notes, usually declining the proffered hand or pleading previous engagements. This culminates in a letter dated 13 July 1944, from Eliot's office at Faber and Faber and in his capacity as an influential editor at that house.

Orwell had already warned Eliot that — as well as being somewhat crumpled by surviving the Nazi bombing of his house — his manuscript of *Animal Farm* possessed a 'meaning which is not an acceptable one at this moment, but I could not agree to make any alterations except a small one at the end which I intended making anyway. Cape or the MOI [Ministry of Information], I am not certain which from the wording of his letter, made the imbecile suggestion that some other animal than the pigs might be made to represent the Bolsheviks . . . '

In his response, Eliot seized upon the same 'imbecile suggestion' and made it his own. Of the novel he wrote:

It ought to excite some sympathy with what the author wants, as well as sympathy with his objections to something: and the positive point of view, which I take to be generally Trotskyite, is not convincing . . . And after all,

> your pigs are far more intelligent than the other animals,
> and therefore the best qualified to run the farm — in fact,
> there couldn't have been an *Animal Farm* at all without
> them: so that what was needed (someone might argue)
> was not more communism but more public-spirited pigs.

The fatuity of this was not as extreme as that of the Dial
Press in New York (which returned the manuscript with the
astonishing comment that animal stories were not a commercial proposition in the USA — this at a time when the
USA was already the domain of Walt Disney). And nor was
it as poltroonishly cowardly as the letter from Jonathan
Cape, which frankly admitted to taking advice from 'an important official in the Ministry of Information' — see Chapter 7 below — and added that 'the choice of pigs as the ruling caste will no doubt give offence to many people, and
particularly to anyone who is a bit touchy, as undoubtedly
the Russians are'. That at least had the merit of candour. The
straightforwardly 'left-wing' Victor Gollancz had of course
refused to publish the book on clear ideological grounds. It
eventually saw print in a very limited edition brought out by
Secker & Warburg, for an advance of £45.

However, there was, as Orwell already knew, an alternative political culture in the ruins of post-fascist and semi-
Stalinized Europe. And it was not long before he heard from
it. In April 1946 he received a letter from a Ukrainian
refugee named Ihor Szewczenko, who was working among
the many ex-prisoners of war and 'displaced persons' scattered in camps across Germany. Though he later rose to become Professor of Byzantine Studies at Harvard, modifying

his name to Ševčenko, this man was at the time a stateless refugee who had taught himself English by listening to the BBC. He wrote:

> For several occasions I translated different parts of 'Animal Farm' ex abrupto. Soviet refugees were my listeners. The effect was striking. They approved of almost all of your interpretations. They were profoundly affected by such scenes as that of animals singing 'Beasts of England' on the hill. Here I saw, that in spite of their attention being primarily drawn on detecting 'concordances' between the reality they lived in and the tale, they very vividly reacted to the 'absolute' values of the book, to the tale 'types', to the underlying convictions of the author and so on. Besides, the mood of the book seems to correspond with their own actual state of mind.

In a subsequent letter, Szewczenko gave Orwell some information about his potential audience, supposing that he should agree to a Ukrainian edition of the book. These former camp-inmates and soldiers, he said, had turned against 'the counter-revolutionary Bonapartism [of] Stalin and the Russian nationalistic exploitation of the Ukrainian people; their conviction is, that the revolution will contribute to the full national development. Britain's socialistic effort (which they take literally) is of foremost interest and importance, they say. Their situation and past, causes them to sympathise with Trotskyites, although there are several differences between them . . . AF is not being published by Ukrainian Joneses.' Looking back on the episode many years later,

Szewczenko wrote that 'those post-war days, combined with the Soviet domination of Poland, witnessed a rapprochement between left-wing or liberal Polish intellectuals and their (few) Ukrainian counterparts — for both sides realised that they had been gobbled up by the same animal'.

Thus, the survivors of the Ukrainian famine, and the purges, and the Nazi invasion and the war, and the subsequent extension of Stalinism into Eastern Europe, were able to decipher the meaning of the pigs (and of the name Napoleon) without any undue difficulty, a task of interpretation that had defeated conservatism's most deft and subtle literary critic. Orwell wrote his only introduction to the novel specially for the Ukrainian edition, and was besieged at the same time by offers to translate it into Latvian, Serbian and other languages. (He instructed his agent to make no charge for these publications.) The fate of the Ukrainian edition was a sad one on the whole. It reached a certain number of readers, but most of the copies were seized and impounded by the American military authorities in Germany, who turned them over to the Red Army for destruction. It was not only the British Ministry of Information which regarded Stalin's *amour-propre* as the chief object of propitiation in those days.

A closing observation: both Malcolm Muggeridge and Herbert Read wrote to Orwell that, while they had relished the Swiftian and satirical elements of *Animal Farm*, their young children had enjoyed it for its own sake as (in the words of its ironic subtitle) 'a fairy story'. That was a rare tribute to authorship, and may help explain the continuing fascination and popularity of the tale. So it is even odder that the author of 'Old Possum' was so obtuse as to miss the point. However, power-worship was at least as strong on the Right as on the Left in the post-war period, and partook of the same kinds of cynical pseudo-realism. And it was precisely this refusal of power-worship and pseudo-realism that was to furnish Orwell with his other great antagonist on the Right — the figure of James Burnham.

Somewhat forgotten today, James Burnham in his time was perhaps the most decisive of those American intellectuals who gave shape and definition to the ideology of the Cold War. His formation might be called a classical one; he was an ex-Stalinist who had for a while associated himself with Leon Trotsky, before abandoning socialism altogether and becoming a chief theorist of the idea of America as an empire. His book *The Managerial Revolution* was a massive wartime bestseller, prefiguring most of the volumes since written, by Daniel Bell or Francis Fukuyama, about the 'end of ideology'. When William Buckley began his highly successful magazine *National Review*, giving an intellectual patina to the utterances of Senator Joseph McCarthy, Burnham contributed a regular column entitled 'Third World War', in which he urged Americans to understand that they were involved in a global life-or-death conflict with atheist Communism. This third world war, he maintained, had already begun. It began at Christmas 1944, when British soldiers opened fire on a Communist demonstration in the central square of newly liberated Athens. Shortly before his death in 1987, Burnham was awarded the Medal of Freedom by President Ronald Reagan, as the godfather of anti-Communism.

Orwell did not live to see McCarthyism (and he had been sharply critical of the British policy in Athens, which he saw as imposing an unwanted reactionary monarchy on the Greeks). But he disliked and distrusted James Burnham's grand theories from the very beginning, and quite evidently drew upon them for his bleak prediction of a tripolar and militarized world in *Nineteen Eighty-Four*.

The first thing that Orwell noticed about Burnham was the slightly sinister purpleness of his style. Here is an example, taken from an ostensible critique of Stalin in Burnham's essay 'Lenin's Heir':

> Stalin proves himself a 'great man,' in the grand style. The accounts of the banquets, staged in Moscow for the visiting dignitaries, set the symbolic tone. With their enormous menus of sturgeon, and roasts, and fowl, and sweets; their streams of liquor; the scores of toasts with which they end; the silent, unmoving secret police behind each guest; all against the winter background of the starving multitudes of besieged Leningrad; the dying millions at the front; the jammed concentration camps; the city crowds kept by their minute rations just at the edge of life; there is little trace of dull mediocrity or the hand of Babbitt. We recognise, rather, the tradition of the most spectacular of the Tsars, of the Great Kings of the Medes and Persians, of the Khanate of the Golden Horde, of the banquet we assign to the gods of the Heroic Ages in tribute to the insight that insolence, and indifference, and brutality on such a scale remove beings from the human level.

Orwell was not mistaken, surely, in detecting here a tinge of vicarious admiration. And how often one was to notice, during the Cold War, a sort of Western penis-envy for the ruthlessness of Soviet methods, coupled with incantations about the relative 'decadence', even tendency to suicide, displayed by the effete democracies. In his 1946 pamphlet on Burnham, published by the Socialist Book Centre, Orwell made the simple but essential point that totalitarian states were much weaker than their iron-jawed propaganda had suggested. By repressing the intelligentsia and silencing public opinion, as well as by promoting the ethereal claims of supreme and absolute but actually quite mediocre 'Great Leaders', they not only made themselves vulnerable to spectacular blunders, but also made it near-impossible for those calamities to be identified or corrected. The classic case in point would be Hitler's decision to invade Russia while still engaged in warfare with Great Britain and potentially the United States; Stalin's inability to foresee his adversary's fatal blunder makes a neat counterpart. Burnham's predictions in all these cases had been utterly falsified by events, because his exaggerated respect for brute force repeatedly led him astray.

Orwell might have pointed out that Burnham's rhetoric was a debased rhetorical carry-over from his previous Leninism. He did instance this distinctly Leninist excerpt from *The Managerial Revolution*:

> There is no historical law that polite manners and 'justice' shall conquer. In history there is always the question of *whose* manners and *whose* justice. A rising social class and

a new order of society have got to break through the old moral codes just as they must break through the old economic and political institutions. Naturally, from the point of view of the old, they are monsters. If they win, they take care in due time of manners and morals.

Once again, one can detect a distinct relish here, on Burnham's part. Orwell largely confined himself to puncturing the mesmerizing grandiosity of the prose. Burnham had shifted his earlier admiration of Nazism to an over-estimation of Stalinism, but he had changed ships on a falling tide. In a passage of extreme prescience, extraordinary for 1946 when the prestige of Stalin in the West was at its zenith, Orwell wrote:

It is too early to say in just what way the Russian regime will destroy itself . . . But at any rate, the Russian regime will either democratise itself, or it will perish. The huge, invincible, everlasting slave empire of which Burnham appears to dream will not be established, or, if established, will not endure, because slavery is no longer a stable basis for human society.

In the event, as we know, the attempt at democratization was the proximate cause of the regime's demise.

Burnham was right, as Orwell conceded, in his analysis of the autonomous role played by bureaucracy and the managerial class; he had adapted the early work of Machiavelli and his later emulators such as Mosca, Michels and Pareto (some of them sympathizers of Mussolini's 'corporate' version of fascism). Indeed, Orwell himself had been extremely quick to see the implication, of a world run by unaccountable experts and technicians, that was contained in the advent of nuclear weaponry.

Orwell did not mean to suggest that the choices — between democratizing and perishing — were exclusive. He thought there was a third alternative, namely the mutual and absolute destruction of all systems (and all non-combatants) by atomic warfare. But though he often wrote about this in the morbidly fatalistic way that was to become commonplace a decade or so after his death, he also saw the threat of nuclearism as a danger to the present as well as the future. Indeed, he cited Burnham in his very first essay on the subject — the essay in which he launched the phrase 'cold war'. For Orwell, the advent of a super-weapon implied also the advent of a caste of nuclear administrators, who could exert near-absolute power by virtue merely of the *latent* effect of their warheads. Thus, in parallel with his decided view that the Soviet Union deserved to collapse and would collapse, he felt the premonitory menace of the arms race, which was the horse running in tandem with the ideological Cold War, and of the 'military-industrial complex' to which President Eisenhower gave a memorable name in 1961. But of the Cold War as an ideology, the arms race as a practice, and the military-industrial complex as an entity, James Burnham remained a devotee to the end of his days, fulfilling some of his own darkest predictions about the fate of intellectuals.

In the haunted and febrile years of the late 1940s, when new fears about nuclear fission competed with fears of Stalinism and were superimposed upon the other disillusionments of the 1930s, a number of formerly pacifistic intellectuals actually proposed a preventive nuclear war with the USSR. Among these were Bertrand Russell, Orwell's co-editor at *Polemic*, and John Middleton Murry, the ex-husband of Katherine Mansfield and Orwell's former literary patron at the *Adelphi*. They thought that the temporary Western advantage in nuclear armaments should be employed to coerce or to destroy the Russian bear. Orwell would have none of this. Having been through the intense battles over Spain and Munich, and having understood them more clearly than many fellow-travellers, he did not think there was any facile analogy to be drawn with 'appeasement', the preferred metaphor of instant Cold-Warriors from 1948 onwards. Nor could he countenance the use of weapons of mass slaughter and destruction. Even those who believe that the arms race ended the Cold War in 1989, by wearing out the Soviet economy, presumably do not wish in retrospect that such weapons had been used in 1948. Among other things, such an act would have destroyed the human beings who did, eventually, bring about the very change that so few had predicted.

At the approach of 1984, that arbitrary year which inevitably became a commemorative occasion, there was a freshet of books and essays revisiting *Nineteen Eighty-Four*. Among these was a celebrated cover story in *Harper's* magazine in New York, garnished with a portrait of Orwell and the bold caption: 'If Orwell Were Alive Today'. It was written by Norman Podhoretz, then the editor of *Commentary* magazine and a vociferous convert both to extreme Reaganism and extreme Zionism, a combination known as 'neo-conservative' in the reigning American vernacular. When *Nineteen Eighty-Four* had come out in 1950, Henry Luce's *Life* magazine had hailed it for exposing the essential totalitarianism of FDR's National Recovery Act and Tennessee Valley Authority, and used it to excoriate 'those fervent New Dealers in the United States [who] often seemed to have the secret hope that the depression mentality of the 1930s, source of their power and excuse for their experiments, would never end'. This image — of Eleanor Roosevelt's sensible shoes crashing down on a human face, forever — was hardly more absurd than Mr Podhoretz's view that George Orwell would, if alive, be standing shoulder to shoulder with none other than himself (William Buckley at the other shoulder and Henry Kissinger lurking potently behind).

I was fascinated by this essay, for two reasons. First, it admired Orwell mainly for his shortcomings (citing with approval his ill-natured remarks on homosexuals, for instance, though not his occasional lapses about Jews). Second, it was incapable of quoting him accurately, let alone fairly. Just like Raymond Williams, Podhoretz was not above taking a remark made by Orwell in the second person and rendering it in the first person: thus when Orwell described a certain crude view of modern warfare as being 'if someone drops a bomb on your mother, go and drop two bombs on his mother', Podhoretz excerpted the slogan and put it in Orwell's own mouth. I happened to be the person chosen by the editor of the magazine to reply, and I observed of this distortion that it would be fun to read Podhoretz's review of Swift's *Modest Proposal,* replete no doubt with rich approval of the stewing of Irish babies.

The great conservative need of that hour was the rallying of waverers to the 'Star Wars' missile programme and against European scepticism; Podhoretz pressed Orwell into service in this way, by quoting as follows from an essay written in

1947 about those who were faced with a confrontation between two superpowers:

> It will not do to give the usual quibbling answer, 'I refuse
> to choose.' . . . We are no longer strong enough to stand
> alone and . . . we shall be obliged, in the long run, to sub-
> ordinate our policy to that of one Great Power or another.

What Orwell had actually written, in his essay *In Defence of
Comrade Zilliacus*, was this:

> It will not do to give the usual quibbling answer, 'I refuse
> to choose.' In the end the choice may be forced upon us.
> We are no longer strong enough to stand alone, and if
> we fail to bring a Western European union into being, we
> shall be obliged, in the long run, to subordinate our pol-
> icy to that of one Great Power or the other.

Earlier that same year he had written:

> In the end, the European peoples may have to accept
> American domination as a way of avoiding domination
> by Russia, but they ought to realize, while there is yet
> time, that there are other possibilities.

And in another 1947 essay he concluded:

> Therefore a socialist United States of Europe seems to me
> the only worthwhile political objective today.

The curious modernity of that thought — of course Orwell might very well have been alive in 1984, a perhaps rather curmudgeonly eighty-one-year-old — might or might not have been modified by time or experience. However, it was the very thought which Podhoretz sought to mask behind his own clumsy ellipses, amounting as they did to flat-out distortion. And all in the name of Orwellian values . . .

It is undoubtedly true that Orwell possessed many conservative instincts, not to say prejudices. As I have argued, he spent his life trying to reason himself out of them. Sometimes his upbringing or his innate pessimism triumphed over his conscious efforts — this seems to have happened quite often when he was ill or depressed — and he would vent some cliché about Jews being money-makers or literary types being queers. (The remark that won Podhoretz's gleeful approval was the one about 'so-called artists who spend on sodomy what they have gained by sponging', a coarse aside about the associates of his lifelong friend Cyril Connolly.) Charles Dickens — a man who really was much more conservative than he seemed — was described by Orwell in a famous and too-lenient review as:

> one of those writers who are well worth stealing. Even the burial of his body in Westminster Abbey was a species of theft, if you come to think of it.
>
> When Chesterton wrote his introductions to the Everyman Edition of Dickens's works, it seemed quite natural to him to credit Dickens with his own highly individual brand of medievalism, and more recently a

Marxist writer, Mr T. A. Jackson, has made spirited efforts to turn Dickens into a bloodthirsty revolutionary. The Marxist claims him as 'almost' a Marxist, the Catholic claims him as 'almost a Catholic' . . .

The body-snatching of Orwell, however, is a much more specialized task and probably should not be attempted by any known faction. Least of all, perhaps, should it be undertaken by Tories of any stripe. George Orwell was conservative about many things, but not about politics.

4

Orwell and America

Some leftists and nationalists in Europe and Canada, and even more people south of the Rio Grande, object to the use of the term 'America' to denote the USA. They prefer to say 'the US' or 'the United States', even though Mexico and El Salvador — for example — are formally entitled *Los Estados Unidos de Mexico* and *Los Estados Unidos de El Salvador*, so that the distinction becomes one with little real difference. The point is a simple one: 'America' is larger as an idea and as a geography than the fifty states of the Union.

But mention 'the American revolution' and you encounter very little argument about terminology. It may well have been Thomas Paine, one of the more intense radicals of 1776, who first employed the phrase 'United States of America' to prefigure a republic that would be more than thirteen

ex-colonies. It was certainly he who proposed the Lousiana
Purchase to Thomas Jefferson, thus helping to double the
size of the country (while vainly hoping to exclude slavery
from the new dominion).

Because of its long alliance with France, and because of
its ancestry in the English revolution of the 1640s, the
American revolution fully deserves its place in the pedigree
of radical upheavals. It has had its full share of contradictions
and negations — its original proclamation by slave holders
who insisted that 'all men are created equal' is one of the first
affirmations on record that some are more equal than others.
But as the third millennium gets under way, and as the Russian and Chinese and Cuban revolutions drop below the
horizon, it is possible to argue that the American revolution,
with its promise of cosmopolitan democracy, is the only
'model' revolution that humanity has left to it.

Orwell was an admirer and student of Paine, himself an
early pattern of the modest self-employed self-publishing
truth-teller. But he exhibited a curious blind spot when it
came to Paine's adopted country. He never visited the United
States and showed little curiosity about it. He was suspicious
of its commercial and mercenary culture, somewhat resentful
of its imperial ambitions, and somewhat fastidious about its
sheer scale and vulgarity. America, in other words, is the grand
exception to Orwell's prescience about the century in which
he lived.

This picture is not without its measure of light and
shade. Like many critics of his day, Orwell took fairly easy
pot-shots at the violence and crassness of American comics

and pulp fiction. His preoccupation with sadism took the form of elevated concern about the nastiness of certain magazines intended for children, which he contrasted with the relative wholesomeness of British 'Boys' Weeklies' and connected to the gangster ethic then becoming fashionable at the movies. If Al Capone were an Englishman, he once wrote rather haughtily, he would not be in jail just for tax evasion.

However, he tried to avoid snobbery and insularity, writing in a guarded manner of Henry Miller's *Tropic of Cancer*, in November 1935, that 'the American language is less flexible and refined than the English, but it has more life in it, perhaps'. That final qualifier expresses an ambivalence which he never quite overcame and which is, perhaps, insuperable even for an admirer of American culture. In April 1936 he quoted a scene of cruelty and violence from a cheap American novel and added:

> This kind of disgusting rubbish (hailed as 'genius' when it comes in a slightly more refined form from Hemingway) is growing commoner and commoner. Some of the three-penny 'Yank Mags' which you buy at Woolworth's now consist of nothing else. Please notice the sinister change that has come over an important sub-department of English fiction. There was, God knows, enough physical brutality in the novels of Fielding, Meredith, Charles Reade, etc., but
> > 'our masters then
> > Were still, at least, our countrymen'
> In the old-style English novel you knocked your man down and then chivalrously waited for him to get up before

knocking him down again; in the modern American version he is no sooner down than you take the opportunity of jumping on his face.

This almost parodically John-Bullish sentiment — complete with romantic insert from Byron — was contrasted a month later by a review which began:

Why is it that the typical English novel is staid to the point of primness and the typical American novel is bursting with noise, 'action' and physical violence? Ultimately, I think, because in America the tradition of nineteenth-century freedom is still alive, though no doubt the reality is as dead as it is here.

In England life is subdued and cautious. Everything is governed by family ties, social status and the difficulty of earning a living, and these things are so important that no novelist can forget them. In America they either do not operate or it is the convention for novelists to leave them out. Hence the hero of an American novel is presented not as a cog in the social machine, but as an individual working out his own salvation with no inhibitions and no sense of responsibility.

Orwell's brief career as a film reviewer for *Time and Tide* in the early years of the Second World War did not represent his finest critical hour but it did illustrate the same duality in his approach to the United States. He deplored the grossness of the product ('the usual machine-made mansion of the

American film') while extolling 'the immense technical superiority of the Americans, their understanding of what is and is
not impressive, their intolerance of amateurishness generally'.
He would also utter the occasional growl about the relative
immunity of America from the rigours of war. However at
about this time — and as another instance of that strange
serendipity whereby people who should find each other actually do manage to do so — he became the London correspondent of *Partisan Review.* This magazine and its editors had
undergone a revulsion from Stalinism very similar to Orwell's
own, men like Philip Rahv and Dwight Macdonald were his
transatlantic co-thinkers. Orwell's wartime letters to *Partisan
Review* were the intellectuals' equivalent of Edward R. Mur-
row's broadcasts from London on CBS: they gave a sense of
immediacy and solidarity. They also compelled Orwell for the
first time to take an American audience into account.

It was in one of these letters, in March 1942, that Orwell
published a sort of disguised self-criticism in a review of
anti-American attitudes in England:

> English cultural feelings towards America are complicated
> but can be defined fairly accurately. In the middle class,
> the people who are *not* anti-American are the declassed
> technician type (people like radio engineers) and the
> younger intelligentsia. Up till about 1930 nearly all 'culti-
> vated' people loathed the U.S.A., which was regarded as
> the vulgariser of England and Europe. The disappearance
> of this attitude was probably connected with the fall of
> Latin and Greek from their dominant position as school

subjects. The younger intellectuals have no objection to
the American language and tend to have a masochistic attitude towards the U.S.A., which they believe to be richer
and more powerful than Britain. Of course it is exactly
this that excites the jealousy of the ordinary patriotic middle class. I know people who automatically switch off the
radio as soon as any American news comes on, and
the most banal English film will always get middle-class
support because 'it's such a relief to get away from those
American voices.' Americans are supposed to be boastful,
bad-mannered and worshippers of money, and are also
suspected of plotting to inherit the British Empire.

(Orwell forgot that last bit when he muttered, shortly after
the war, about the new American empire that was 'advancing
behind a smoke-screen of novelists'.) In other words, he
could reprobate simplistic anti-Americanism in others even
when not completely eliminating it in himself. This ambigu-
ity, as I've already tried to point out, occurs in almost all his
discussions of prejudice.

In one of his letters to *Partisan Review*, Orwell gave his
office address and home telephone number and issued an
open invitation to any readers of the magazine to come and
call upon him. Not very many GIs were *Partisan Review* sub-
scribers, but this fraternal gesture did attract a few visitors. At
the same time, he was ventilating a subject which gave rise to
great nervousness on the part of the British authorities:

Even if you steer clear of Piccadilly with its seething
swarms of drunks and whores, it is difficult to go anywhere

in London without having the feeling that Britain is now Occupied Territory. The general consensus of opinion seems to be that the only American soldiers with decent manners are the Negroes . . . Before the war there was no popular anti-American feeling in this country. It all dates from the arrival of the American troops, and it is made vastly worse by the tacit agreement never to discuss it in print.

Orwell's egalitarian instinct made him chafe at the grotesque difference in pay between the American and British soldiers ('the whole American army is financially in the middle class') while his intuitive patriotism was aroused through the depiction of the stage and screen Englishman in America as:

a chinless ass with a title, a monocle and a habit of saying 'Haw, haw.' This legend is believed in by relatively responsible Americans, for example by the veteran novelist Theodore Dreiser, who remarks in a public speech that 'the British are horse-riding aristocratic snobs.' (Forty-six million horse-riding snobs!)

Hostile though it is, the mention of Dreiser is a clue to the way in which Orwell tried to resolve this dilemma within himself. He always took American literature seriously (something that was by no means taken for granted among his contemporaries), and he came to the conclusion that its success as a new literature had something to do with liberty. Of course his tendency was to identify this with the incomplete struggle for liberty, rather than a mere grant or promise of it

— an excellent BBC programme which he produced on the
subject in November 1942 lays emphasis on the grittier work
of James T. Farrell, John Steinbeck and Archibald MacLeish.
But the broadcast was not only concerned with oppressed
immigrants and hard-driven labourers; it considered Eliot's
Prufrock with some care, gave honourable mentions to Whitman and Henry James, and contained a long extract from
Herman Melville's *White-Jacket*, read aloud by Orwell himself. The West Indian authoress Una Marson was invited to
consider what were still called 'negro writers', and to present
her own work. With William Empson and Herbert Read
and Mulk Raj Anand as his co-readers, Orwell also discussed
Bret Harte on Dickens and the vagaries of Mark Twain.

American literature begins with Mark Twain, as Hemingway generously if uncontroversially observed, and it's pleas-
antly surprising to find Orwell proposing himself (unsuccess-
fully) as Twain's biographer in a letter to his agent in 1932. In
1943 he wrote a long essay on Twain instead, in which he
identified the essence of a frontier style which, for all the
faults and even fraudulence of its legend, evoked a real world
where 'at least it was not the case that a man's destiny was settled from his birth. The "log cabin to White House" myth
was true while the free land lasted. In a way, it was for this
that the Paris mob had stormed the Bastille, and when one
reads Mark Twain, Bret Harte and Whitman it is hard to feel
that their effort was wasted.' Orwell was one of the few English critics to keep in mind a memory that the twentieth
century had already done much to distort and overlay — an
English folk memory of the time when America was the

promised land of freedom and equality. He even attacked his beloved Charles Dickens, on the centennial of *Martin Chuzzlewit* in 1944, for writing the novel that set out to belittle and defame this noble idea. *Martin Chuzzlewit* is by no means the best of Dickens's novels, even in the opinion of his staunchest defenders, but it took Orwell to say that the pages were 'as though Dickens were dissolving into lukewarm treacle' and that 'the American chapters are a good example of Dickens's habit of telling small lies in order to emphasise what he regards as a big truth'. This thought in turn prompts the following comparison:

> The mental atmosphere of the American interlude is one that has since become familiar to us in the books written by British travellers to Soviet Russia. Some of these report that everything is good, others that everything is bad, but nearly all share the same propagandist outlook. A hundred years ago America, 'the land of the free,' had rather the same place in the European imagination that Soviet Russia has now, and 'Martin Chuzzlewit' is the 1844 equivalent of André Gide's *Retour de l'URSS*. But it is a sign of the changing temper of the world that Dickens's attack, so much more violent and unfair than Gide's, could be so quickly forgiven.

In 1945 Orwell was asked by Fredric Warburg to prepare a reader's report on the novels of F. Scott Fitzgerald, and by the BBC Latin American service to write a review of Benjamin Franklin's autobiography. He didn't complete either of these commissions. In the same year, however, he did write a most perceptive appreciation of the life and work of Jack London. Orwell's health was beginning to fail him badly at this time, and it can be conjectured that there is a certain envy in his admiration for London's virility and ruthlessness, his 'commanding character and powerful physique'. This, combined with the appeal of North America's immense space and fierce individualism, evidently struck a chord in the ailing and enfeebled man.

Reviewing a selection of popular fiction from the United States in the following year, Orwell wrote that 'one other imaginary country that I acquired early in life was called America. If I pause on the word "America," and, deliberately putting aside the existing reality, call up my childhood vision of it, I see two pictures'. . . . There follows a very deft freehand sketch of the worlds of Tom Sawyer and Uncle Tom, with the conclusion that: 'The civilisation of nineteenth-century America was capitalist civilisation at its best.' Only a few months earlier, however, he had written to his agent to say that while he would be happy to review for the *New Yorker* (which he later did): 'As to visiting the USA, I have never had the slightest idea of doing so, and I don't know how the rumour can have got about.' It seemed that it was enough to visit the country in his mind.

As the curtain was descending, his mind almost changed. Philip Rahv wrote to him from *Partisan Review*, urging him to come and visit his many American admirers. Acutely aware of the state of Orwell's health, he added that there were many ideal climates in the United States, well-suited to his tubercular condition. For a brief time, Orwell contemplated spending some time in the South, and writing a series of reports about everyday life in Dixie. But in the end, he was too weak to venture on any such voyage. It's impossible to contemplate the unrealized project of Orwell on the Mississippi without a piercing sense of loss.

The relationship between health and the United States persisted in a more banal form; the streptomycin that might have healed his lungs was only manufactured in America and there were bureaucratic, as well as financial, obstacles to obtaining it in England. Orwell enlisted the help of David Astor to try to gain access to a regular supply of this medicine. Once again, it was too little and too late; this correspondence has the same pathos as his letters to Dwight Macdonald (by then editing his own brilliant one-man review *Politics,* to which Orwell contributed) begging him to acquire a pair of shoes suitable for a large-footed man in a time and place of rationing and scarcity. The final American reference I can find is in a letter to Astor very near the end, in July 1949, in which Orwell asks: 'Have you read "The Naked and The Dead"? It's awfully good, the best war book of the last war yet.' Here is another brief frustrating glimpse of a potentially fruitful engagement that never quite matured.

The innovative medicine that might have saved him, the contacts with fellow-dissidents that were tentatively made but not reinforced by personal contact, the unexplored avenues of literature and language — the American subject was in every sense Orwell's missed opportunity.

5

Orwell and 'Englishness'
The Antinomies of St George

The phrase 'quintessentially English', so often attached to Orwell's name, would fairly certainly have aroused his scorn. Few of his fictional scenes are more plainly autobiographical than the opening chapter of *Keep the Aspidistra Flying*, which recreates his own time as a bookshop assistant in South End Green, Hampstead. Here, the wretched underling Gordon Comstock is compelled to be civil to the vapid literary snob, Mrs Penn:

> 'What I feel, Mr Comstock, is that there's something so *big* about Galsworthy. He's so broad, so universal, and yet at the same time so thoroughly English in spirit, so *human*. His books are real *human* documents.'

'And Priestley, too,' said Gordon. 'I think Priestley's such an awfully fine writer, don't you?'

'Oh, he is! So big, so broad, so human. And so essentially English! . . . I wonder whether you have Hugh Walpole's latest book?' said Mrs Penn. 'I feel in the mood this week for something epic, something *big*. Now Walpole, you know, I consider a really *great* writer. I put him second only to Galsworthy. There's something so *big* about him. And yet he's so human with it.'

'And so essentially English,' said Gordon.

'Oh, of course! So essentially English!'

But not even this rather excessive sarcasm is sufficient to deter Orwell's Albion brigade. Some of the Albion faction even point to his spirited defence of P. G. Wodehouse, as showing the essential kinship that links our national literary treasures. They rather understate the fact that Wodehouse was to all intents and purposes an American, as well as the fact that, at the time of Orwell's defence, Mr Wodehouse was being pelted with calumny by every red-faced bully and roast-beef demagogue in the sceptr'd isle, a campaign of witless defamation that enjoyed official encouragement and which required the passage of many decades before it was redressed.

As the twentieth century expired, the 'condition of England' question revived in a very acute form. With the United Kingdom devolving (or deliquescing, according to taste and interpretation) the assertion of Scottish and Welsh and Irish nationhood was met in the southern nation with an efflorescence of the flag of St George. Sometimes an emblem on pubs or taxis, or on the brawny limbs of soccer fans, its reappearance was often a symptom of insecurity, both about the internal state of the kingdom and the external challenge represented by the idea of 'Europe'. In this context, the number of easy references to Orwell mounted steadily. The last Tory Prime Minister of the century, John Major, was to the fore. Seeking to reassure a Conservative audience in April 1993, he reiterated a commitment to the theory and practice of the 'European' idea, but insisted:

> That is the best of Britain and it is part of our distinctive and unique contribution to Europe. Distinctive and unique as Britain will remain in Europe. Fifty years from now Britain will still be the country of long shadows on county grounds, warm beer, invincible green suburbs, dog lovers and pools fillers and — as George Orwell said — 'old maids bicycling to holy communion through the morning mist' and — if we get our way — Shakespeare still read even in school. Britain will survive unamendable in all essentials.

Mr Major thought well enough of this trope to include it in his later autobiography. And he was confident enough of the resonance of the name to return to it in his speech to the Conservative Party conference in the autumn of 1995:

> I think Labour has been reading *Nineteen Eighty-Four* — the book that introduced 'doublethink'. You remember — doublethink is the trick of holding two contradictory beliefs at the same time — and accepting both. It was the brain-child of another public-school-educated Socialist.

His name was George Orwell. But actually it wasn't. That
was his pen name. His real name was Eric. His surname?
You've guessed it. It was Blair. Eric Blair. He changed his
name. I can't say the same thing about my opposite number. He's changed everything else. His politics. His principles. His philosophy. But to the best of my belief he hasn't
changed his name.

Loud cheers and laughter. It will be noticed that Mr Major
was not as generous in his attribution on the second occasion
as he had been on the first — Orwell has morphed from a
synonym for patriotism into a 'public-school-educated Socialist'. This is a protean style that even the chameleon Tony
Blair himself might wish to emulate. But it helps express the
ambivalence that the English feel about Orwell, and thus the
ambivalence that Orwell himself felt about the English (or,
as John Major, saddled with Unionism and the flag, was
obliged to call them, 'the British').

Orwell was something of a sceptic about Britishness and
the Union. Though he barely mentions the Welsh, and touches
on Ireland only in the first line of 'Beasts of England' and in
one or two backward glances at the atrocities of the Black and
Tans, he wrote at some length about the potential for a resur-
gence of Scottish nationalism, a movement which he had
learned about from the elementary technique of studying, and
taking seriously, the letters he received from readers. His references to the monarchy are few and generally contemptuous.
Realizing that it had suffered a near-mortal blow from the abdi-
cation, he felt it had gained ground during the war and would

probably recover something of its former position if it could manage 'a really long reign', of the sort which actually began shortly after the death both of himself and the last King George.

There are a number of near-misses in Orwell's career, which can only make one wish that the original fixtures had come off. In Paris after the Liberation, he waited in vain in the *Café Deux Magots* for Albert Camus to turn up, and finally left in disappointment. (This fills one with the same sense of sadness as the aborted rendezvous between Marx and Darwin, or Evelyn Waugh and H. L. Mencken, or Alexander Solzhenitsyn and Vladimir Nabokov.) And how might it have been if Orwell had got together with Philip Rahv or Dwight Macdonald or Mary McCarthy? However, there is one encounter that actually did take place, yet which failed to amount to anything. On 23 May 1941, Orwell was invited to speak at Oxford University, on the topic of 'Literature and Totalitarianism', to an evening meeting sponsored by the Democratic Socialist Club and the English Club. In his capacity as treasurer of the latter, the young Philip Larkin helped host a dinner afterwards at a 'not-so-good hotel', conscious of the fact that Dylan Thomas had been more expensively entertained at the rather superior Randolph. 'I suppose it was,' as Larkin later observed, 'my first essay in practical criticism.'

Orwell had evoked 'England' in the following fashion in the closing pages of *Homage to Catalonia*:

The railway-cuttings smothered in wild flowers, the deep meadows where the great shining horses browse and meditate, the slow-moving streams bordered by willows, the green bosoms of the elms, the larkspurs in the cottage gardens; and then the huge peaceful wilderness of outer London, the barges on the miry river, the familiar streets, the posters telling of cricket matches and Royal weddings, the men in bowler hats, the pigeons in Trafalgar Square, the red buses, the blue policemen — all sleeping the deep, deep sleep of England, from which I sometimes fear that we shall never wake until we are jerked out of it by the roar of bombs.

And Larkin was much later to phrase it like this in his poem 'Going, Going' in 1972:

> And that will be England gone,
> The shadows, the meadows, the lanes,
> The guildhalls, the carved choirs.
> There'll be books; it will linger on
> In galleries; but all that remains
> For us will be concrete and tyres.

It would be impossible to prove this, but there is something about 'Englishness', especially as this quality is inscribed upon the landscape and in the ancient towns, that both lends itself to melancholy and pessimism, and borrows from these. Both Orwell and Larkin are drawing on the same store of greensward and grey stone; both share an inward conviction that it's too vulnerable and fragile to endure. In their separate ways, Oliver Goldsmith and William Blake knew the same fear. So did Cobbett and Dickens. Giving the Irishman Yeats as his salient example, Orwell said that 'on the whole, the best writers of our time have been reactionary in tendency'. (Larkin told his biographer, Andrew Motion, that his own first literary inspirations were Orwell, Cyril Connolly, and George Bernard Shaw.)

One might pause to notice, also, that Larkin almost evokes *Nineteen Eighty-Four*, both in his image of dreary concrete and in his resigned feeling that only some old volumes and musty pictures will preserve a hint of the vanished idyll. Larkin was a Tory, not to say a reactionary, and his poem was actually commissioned by a Conservative government for a White Paper on the environment. (This did not prevent the Countess of Dartmouth from excising, for political purposes, his earlier lines about how 'On the Business Page, a score/Of spectacled grins approve/Some takeover bid that entails/Five per cent profit [and ten/Per cent more in the estuaries] . . . ') Orwell was a 'public-school-educated Socialist' who did indeed change his name — so that the first name was that of England's patron saint, and the second was that of a river which meanders inoffensively through East Anglia before forming an estuary of its own. The emblematic novel where these two tributaries meet would certainly be, with its dread of modern ugliness and of rural desecration and suburban philistinism, Orwell's *Coming Up for Air*: suburbia vanquishes Arcadia. Larkin's representation of the smug and greedy new Britain as run by 'a cast of crooks and tarts' could have been lifted directly from Orwell at his most sulphurous.

One more comparison may be worth making: Larkin and Orwell showed a very similar attitude to religion. Quite unimpressed by the metaphysical claims of Christianity, Larkin would pause in wayside churches ('Once I am sure there's nothing going on') and, having imbibed the atmosphere, would 'sign the book, donate an Irish sixpence/Reflect the place was not worth stopping for.' Yet his indifference to the ceremonial was matched by a grainy respect for the sense of place, for history, for 'so many dead [that] lie round' and for — his much repeated word in the closing stanza of 'Church Going' — the 'serious'. In *Coming Up for Air*, Orwell's George Bowling is so embarrassed by meeting a clergyman from his boyhood that he cuts short his tour of the ancient church: 'As soon as I decently could I dropped sixpence in the Church Expenses box and bunked.'

Orwell, too, had a rooted dislike for supernatural propaganda, especially in its Roman Catholic form, but possessed a fondness for church architecture and displayed a working knowledge of both Testaments in his writing. The liturgy of Cranmer and King James was dear to him, and in *A Clergyman's Daughter* he cleverly anticipated the fork on which Anglicanism has since impaled itself:

> Nowadays, a clergyman who wants to keep his congregation has only two courses open to him. Either it must be Anglo-Catholicism pure and simple — or rather, pure and not simple; or he must be daringly modern and broad-minded and preach comforting sermons proving that there is no Hell and all good religions are the same.

This seems to anticipate the later obituary written for itself by what George Herbert once so tellingly called 'the sweet mediocrity of our native Church'. There is also the hilarious scene depicting the itinerant 'book-wallah', in *Burmese Days*:

> His system of exchange was that for any book in his bundle you gave him four annas, and *any* other book. Not quite any book, however, for the book-wallah, though analphabetic, had learned to recognise and refuse a Bible.
>
> 'No, sahib,' he would say plaintively, 'no. This book' (he would turn it over disapprovingly in his flat brown hands) 'this book with a black cover and gold letters — this one I cannot take. I know not how it is, but all sahibs are offering me this book, and none are taking it. What can it be that is in this black book? Some evil, undoubtedly.'

Having witnessed pious missionaries acting as the sanctifiers of colonial robbery, and having all his life alluded matter-of-factly to the existence of a post-Christian society, Orwell left very careful instructions about the sort of Anglican funeral that he wanted for himself. His friend Anthony Powell — another writer often identified as 'quintessentially English' — helped with the obsequies at Christ Church, Albany Street:

> It fell to me to choose the hymns: *All people that on earth do dwell* (I felt Orwell would have liked the Old Hundredth, if only for the name); *Guide me, O thou great Redeemer* (chiefly for my own wartime associations, though *Jehovah* is more authentic); *Ten thousand times ten thousand* (Why, I can't remember, perhaps Orwell himself had

talked of the hymn, or because he was in his way a sort of saint, even if not one in sparkling raiment bright). The lesson was from Ecclesiastes, the grinders in the streets, the grasshopper a burden, the silver cord loosed, the wheel broken at the cistern. For some reason George Orwell's funeral service was one of the most harrowing I have ever attended.

Powell, too, was at best a neutral in religious matters, preferring to concentrate his interest on the occult and the pagan (and one might pause here to give credit to Eton College for accommodating both him and George Orwell in the same intake). The only false note in such a finely wrought paragraph comes with the invocation of the 'saint'; unsought and indeed repudiated by Orwell and the cause of much of the irrational resentment against his name.

With David Astor's patrician assistance, Orwell's body was later laid in the churchyard at Sutton Courtenay in Oxfordshire, a patch of 'deep England', deep enough indeed to enclose the nearby grave of Margot Asquith and her husband. As Lady Oxford, Mrs Asquith had caught Orwell's stern attention in June 1940. She had written to the *Daily Telegraph*, observing in what Joyce Cary would have called 'a tumbril remark' that: 'Since most London houses are deserted there is little entertaining . . . in any case, most people have to part with their cooks and live in hotels.' Of this splendid piece of aristocratic callousness Orwell commented in his diary that 'apparently nothing will ever teach these people that the other 99% of the population exist'. England, whose England?

   This takes the Orwell–Larkin comparison about as far as it will go, in the undeclared contest for most symbolic Englishman. (Some have claimed to find, in Orwell's work, an undue interest in whipping and caning and the sexual undertones of corporal punishment; this fascination was Larkin's favourite pornographic recreation as well as, according to legend and a Himalaya of empirical evidence, the distinctive English vice.) But the overt and covert resemblances cease where the actual people of England begin. Larkin, it is fairly safe to say, was not what some Americans call 'a people person'. Devoted and meticulous in private and professional relations, he had no taste for the inhabitants of the island *en masse*, as it were. Nor did he much care for the inhabitants of other countries, whether they stayed where they were or tried to move to England. Larkin was for Enoch Powell; Orwell defended the coloured subjects of the Empire at home and abroad. Larkin mourned the withdrawal from 'East of Suez'; Orwell wanted the whole colonial racket wound up. Larkin famously reprobated family life and reproduction, recoiling especially from 'kiddies'; Orwell thought the English were too scared to breed enough, and keenly wished to become a father himself. Larkin shuddered at the thought of the seaside in 'Going, Going'; Orwell celebrated the brash vigour of Donald McGill's end-of-the-pier postcards. Larkin was a law-and-order type who hated rioters and strikers; Orwell thought the English were too passive and placid, and reserved a particular dislike for policemen.

   Thus, the superficial attitude towards warm beer, brass rubbings, cathedral closes and the distant thwack of willow on leather — the whole repertoire of supposed Englishness and sentiment — is a poor guide to questions of principle. One of the very few texts which Orwell directed his agents and executors to suppress was a wartime pamphlet, written in haste for the British Council and entitled 'The English People'. When consulted today, this little effort holds up quite well. Though calmly and resolutely patriotic, it is by no means uncritical of its subject and makes few concessions to flag waving. But one must conclude that it fell just on the wrong side of the permanent ambivalence which Orwell maintained when it came to his kith and kin.

Partly French on his mother's side to begin with, Orwell spent his formative years seeing the British at their absolute worst. The hellish snobbery and sadism of the prep-school system, and the dirty work of Empire, made indelible scratches on his mind, and furnished him with seams of material he was never to exhaust. Even during the Second World War, in the course of deploring anti-English attitudes in America, he freely conceded that 'we send our worst specimens abroad'. This sort of tension is familiar to anyone who has been embarrassed by fellow-countrymen overseas, or who has felt the contrasting sensation that even the most insufferable family members must be defended from outside criticism. Indeed, Orwell pushed this analogy as far as he could, if not a little further, in his other wartime writings. England was a family with the wrong members in control, he wrote, with rich relations who are horribly kowtowed to, and poor relations who are horribly sat upon. Withal, an awful conspiracy of silence about the source of the family income.

(This map of the clan, by the way, is notable for having no mention of any father in it; a rare giveaway of Orwell's distraught relationship with his own male parent.)

So hostile was Orwell to conventional patriotism, and so horrified by the cynicism and stupidity of the Conservatives in the face of fascism, that he fell for some time into the belief that 'Britain', as such or as so defined, wasn't worth fighting for. In August 1937 he wrote angrily that:

> It is desperately necessary to get people to see through the humbug that is talked about 'fighting against Fascism,' or the next thing we know we shall find ourselves fighting another imperialist war (against Germany) which will be dressed up as a war 'against Fascism', and then another ten million men will be dead before people grasp that Fascism and so-called democracy are Tweedledum and Tweedledee.

With increasing strain, he held on to a version of this view until the war itself was well under way. He even made a number of extremely foolish proposals, to extremely improbable people, for underground resistance to the Churchill government. It was with evident relief that he jettisoned this hopeless position, becoming a sort of post-Trotskyist Home Guarder (see p. 40). This, too, led him into error, as he was later to confess to the readers of *Partisan Review* in the winter of 1944:

> I don't share the average English intellectual's hatred of his own country and am not dismayed by a British victory. But just for the same reason I failed to form a true picture

of political developments. *I hate to see England either hu-
miliated or humiliating anybody else.* I wanted to think
that we would not be defeated, and I wanted to think that
the class distinctions and imperialist exploitation of
which I am ashamed would not return. I over-emphasized
the anti-Fascist character of the war, exaggerated the social changes that were actually occurring; and under-rated
the enormous strength of the forces of reaction. This un-
conscious falsification coloured all my earlier letters to
you . . . [my italics].

Orwell as a writer was forever taking his own temperature.
If the thermometer registered too high or too low, he took
measures to correct matters. He could analyse the hidden as-
sumptions of a Scottish or Jewish joke as readily as he could
write that the British Empire favoured 'gangs of Jews and
Scotchmen'. His defence of English cooking and the English
pub is written in a heartfelt way, but he knew and denounced
the awful tyranny of the national cuisine and the restrictive li-
censing hours. Only on two of the stock images did he take
what might be called a completely conventional view. His long
essay on how to make a proper pot of tea is highly orthodox,
down to the crucial detail of taking the pot to the kettle instead of the kettle to the pot. And he had a strong conviction
that the metric system — which was to become such a toxic issue in England in the early years of this millennium — was
somehow ill-suited to humans, let alone Englishmen.

He conceded that for industrial and scientific purposes
the metric scheme was necessary. However:

> The metric system does not possess, or has not succeeded in
> establishing, a large number of units that can be visualised.
> There is, for instance, effectively no unit between the metre,
> which is more than a yard, and the centimetre, which is less
> than half an inch. In English you can describe someone as
> being five feet three inches high . . . but I have never heard a
> Frenchman say, 'He is a hundred and forty-two centimetres
> high'; it would not convey any visual image.

In the literary aspect of the question, which he naturally did
not neglect, Orwell pointed out that 'the names of the units
in the old system are short homely words which lend themselves to vigorous speech. Putting a quart into a pint pot is a
good image, which could hardly be expressed in the metric
system.' There was also the matter of the literature of the past,
with its miles and furlongs. He wrote this in 1947. Not long
afterwards, he was protesting to his agent that the American
publishers of *Nineteen Eighty-Four* had, at the proof stage,
rendered all his metric measurements into the old form: 'The
use of the metric system was part of the buildup and I don't
want it changed if avoidable.' It's easy to see why. When Winston Smith goes slumming with the proles in Chapter Eight,
he gets into a futile conversation with an addled old man
whose memory — so crucial to Winston — is a wreck except
for unimportant details:

> 'I arst you civil enough, didn't I?' said the old man,
> straightening his shoulders pugnaciously. 'You telling me
> you ain't got a pint mug in the 'ole bleeding boozer?'

'And what in hell's name *is* a pint?' said the barman, leaning forward with the tips of his fingers on the counter.

' 'Ark at 'im. Calls 'isself a barman and don't know what a pint is! Why, a pint's the 'alf of a quart, and there's four quarts to the gallon. 'Ave to teach you the A, B, C next.'

'Never 'eard of 'em,' said the barman shortly. 'Litre and half litre — that's all we serve.'

In this coarse exchange, Orwell succeeds in depicting a sodden deracinated people who have been forcibly alienated from the familiar things that were near and dear to them.

Yet his attention to the smallest inflections of language and words is another of the things which marks Orwell off from the 'Merrie England' school. As English nationalism began to stir again in the early 2000s, a number of polemical writers — my Tory brother Peter among them — began to say that English was a tongue in which it was easier to tell the truth than it was to tell a lie. Peter told me when I pressed him that he thought he had annexed this notion from a novel by Simon Raven. He later changed his mind about this, but either or both of them might have drawn the idea, even subliminally, from another common source:

Speak to us in our own English tongue, the tongue made for telling truth in, tuned already to songs that haunt the hearer like the sadness of spring . . . These are not thoughts for every day, nor words for every company; but

on St George's Eve, in the Society of St George, may we
not fitly think and speak them, to renew and strengthen
in ourselves the resolves and the loyalties which English
reserve keeps otherwise and best in silence?

That was Enoch Powell, addressing the Society of St George
in 1969. (Ignoring his own counsel about native reticence,
he reprinted the rhetoric as the climax to his book *Freedom
and Reality*.)

It is not difficult to guess what Orwell would have made
of such windy prose. Leave alone the high-Jingo element of
Powellism: he had devoted his classic essay 'Politics and the
English Language' to anatomizing the most appalling instances of blather and falsification, all of them in English.
His version of St George was also able and willing to slay national dragons, and to take on — rather than to transmit or
represent — national myths. He may have called his adopted
son Richard Horatio, but he recommended that friends visit
St Paul's Cathedral to view the statues of colonial bishops,
'which will give you a laugh'. His interest in English as a language — aside from its ingenuity in euphemism and propaganda, and its surpassing literary tradition — derived largely
from his prescient conviction that it would become an international tongue, and thus that the task of keeping it relatively unpolluted was a grand human project. In his one
comment on F. R. Leavis's celebrated reading of 'English' as
'The Great Tradition' — a tradition that deliberately excluded such men as Milton — he commented on the proposed canon of George Eliot, Henry James, Joseph Conrad

and Jane Austen, and said that 'two of these "English novelists" are not even English and one of them, Conrad, derives
entirely from French and Russian sources'.

The English question is inextricably bound up with the
countryside, and in a somehow related fashion with the national love of animals. Orwell spent many frugal years running a rural shop in Wallington, Hertfordshire, with a patch
of farm attached to it, and in husbanding some inhospitable
acres on the remote Scottish island of Jura. He had dirt under his fingernails, and an understanding of the rhythms of
nature. Precisely for this reason, he was disinclined to ro-
manticize the cult of the bucolic. Reviewing a book entitled
The Way of A Countryman in 1944, he wrote:

> There is no question that a love of what is loosely called
> 'nature' — a kingfisher flashing down a stream, a bull-
> finch's mossy nest, the caddis-flies in the ditch — is very
> widespread in England, cutting across age-groups and
> even class-distinctions, and attaining in some people an
> almost mystical intensity.
>
> Whether it is a healthy symptom is another matter. It
> arises partly from the small size, equable climate, and var-
> ied scenery of England, but it is also probably bound up
> with the decay of English agriculture. Real rustics are not
> conscious of being picturesque, they do not construct
> bird sanctuaries, they are uninterested in any bird or ani-
> mal that does not affect them directly . . . The fact is that
> those who really have to deal with nature have no cause to
> be in love with it.

He pointed out also the fatal tendency of many rural reveries to picture England as a place with many wild creatures but no people. (And in Jura, he found that keeping pigs could be a loathsome business.)

With another part of his mind, however, Orwell was extremely tender about birds and beasts and flowers and trees. It took him a considerable time before he was able to make full use of this element in the writing of *Animal Farm*, but his Englishness (and also his apartness from Englishness) can both be identified by following this trace. 'Most of the good memories of my childhood, and up to the age of twenty,' he said, 'are in some way connected with animals.' It would be as true to say that some of his worst adult recollections were conditioned in the same way. Rudyard Kipling's British soldier, longing for Mandalay, pauses and repeats himself in wonder when he recalls watching elephants peacefully piling logs as the dusk came on: 'Elephints a-piling teak!' Orwell famously shot a Burmese elephant in a shaming attempt to demonstrate British pluck and resolve in front of a restive crowd; his character Flory in *Burmese Days* has done the same thing (though the circumstances are not specified) and regards his own action in the light of a murder. We know at once that the girl who wins his heart, Elizabeth Lackersteen, is a bad egg. We know it because she is either frightened of animals — in the same way that she is repelled by the Burmese — or else determined to hunt and kill them. (She is 'thrilled' to hear his confessions about the murder of the elephant.) She later suffers well-deserved humiliation at the hands of the detestable Verrall, the very model of the hunting and shooting and polo type, who in his callous way prefers animals to people. This reverse side of the British or English character held no appeal for Orwell; he understood the relationship between sentimentality and brutality and was offended by visitors to impoverished countries who exclaimed about the poor overworked donkeys but barely noticed 'the old woman under her load of sticks'. (In Morocco, he noted and deplored this very blindness in himself.)

In December 2000, Margaret Drabble read a paper entitled 'Of Beasts and Men: Orwell on Beastliness' to the Royal Society of Literature. She began by remarking upon the repetitive use of the word 'beastly', both in his fiction and in his essays. It was evidently a childhood term from which he never parted company. Ms Drabble correctly observed that the word was commonplace in middle-class slang in her own childhood; it was still current if slightly archaic when I was a schoolboy and it meant anything disgusting or boring ('that beastly film'), or anything unkind — as in the now-forgotten ditty 'Don't let's be beastly to the Germans'. (Its opposite, which she might have found worth mentioning, was the word 'decent', another term habitually applied to Orwell both as man and as writer, and yet another of the supposedly 'English virtues'.) It also had a third implication, that of sexual delinquency. To commit 'beastliness' was to befoul the temple of the body, something that, as Orwell discovered at his own prep school, it was appallingly easy to do, or at any rate to be accused of doing.

Orwell habitually deployed the word 'beast' or 'beastly' to summarize anyone or anything he didn't care for. None the

less the anthem 'Beasts of England', retrieved from the golden
past by the old boar Major, singing with eloquence about the
golden future, and rendered so touchingly by the oppressed
farm animals, hints at nothing pejorative in the word 'beast',
any more than I was guilty of lapsing into speciesism when I
employed the word 'brutality' two paragraphs ago. The solu-
tion to this apparent contradiction is, I believe, to be found in
Orwell's sense of proportion. He abhorred cruelty to dumb
creatures but found vegetarianism more than mildly ridiculous. He was very fond of animals but generally represented
fanatical pet-owners as somewhat contemptible. He had a
dog named Marx but kept him engaged in a working farm.
He adored fishing but it's impossible to imagine him bother-
ing to keep a fish in a bowl. He loved the landscape but didn't
want it depopulated — as it had been in English history — to
make room for sheep or pheasants or deer. The parts of 'creation' have their place, but their place is within a whole.

Thus the scheme of *Animal Farm* owes both its depth
and its simplicity to the fact that all animals are not the
same. In a world of anthropomorphic allegory (where all
men are brutes), beasts can be better differentiated. Thus
pigs — despised by Orwell — are at least to be given high
marks for intelligence, while dogs — much admired by Orwell — are exploited, and mutate into enforcers, because of
their famous quality of loyalty. Orwell was influenced by the
writing of Jonathan Swift at an early age, and his fascination
with creaturely metaphors (to say nothing of his obsessive
disgust and his inability to shake off thoughts of the squalid)
owes a good deal to the Dean. The clean honest world of the

Houyhnhnms of *Gulliver's Travels* is partly recreated in *Animal Farm*; the death of the stolid carthorse Boxer exceeds in its pathos — because of Boxer's massive gentle innocence — even the crashing majestic final agony of Orwell's real-life Burmese elephant.

Jean-Paul Sartre — who was regarded with great suspicion by Orwell — once made a telling point about fictional and science-fictional monsters. What we fear, he said, is a creature of great cunning and energy, quite devoid of any moral or mammalian scruple. This, as he went on to say, is an exact description of our very own species in time of war or scarcity. Thus it is perfect, in its way, that the dehumanized torturers of *Nineteen Eighty-Four* demonstrate their purely human ingenuity by devising the punishment of the rats. Just as Orwell could employ a version of the English pastoral — the Manor Farm — to evoke the Gulag and the revolution betrayed, so he could begin with an English version of the Gulag and populate it with only one wild animal in order to induce choking terror.

(A word on the aspidistra. This favoured pot-plant of the landlady and of the living-dead respectable is now so far out of fashion as to make Orwell's fascination with it seem quaint, if not antique. It occurs again and again, not just in its own eponymous novel, but also in *A Clergyman's Daughter*, where an unfrocked vicar is found singing 'Keep the aspidistra flying', to the tune of 'Deutschland Über Alles', among the derelicts in Trafalgar Square. And it is also to be found in *Burmese Days*, where Flory, looking for peace and nature in the jungle, reaches 'an impasse where the path was blocked by large ugly plants like magnified aspidistras'. The original idea of the aspidistra as a fetish came to Orwell by way of Robert Tressell's celebrated proletarian novel *The Ragged-Trousered Philanthropists*, in which a starving carpenter is forced to pawn everything but clings to his potted shrub as an idiotic token of social status. What I suspect is this: for Orwell this grubbed-up and replanted thing was *de-natured*, a pseudo or kitsch version of vegetation masquerading as greenery among the deracinated and the suburban. What he liked and respected, in a phrase, was the real thing.)

We now have a much better idea of our own relationship with, and dependence upon, the natural order. The vandalizing of the rainforests and the unhealthy exploitation of farm animals, with their awful consequences for humans, are at the centre of modern rather than nostalgic concern. Even more salient is the elucidation of the human genome, which actually demonstrates what has long been intuitively obvious — our kinship with fellow-creatures and other species. In this scientific sense, Orwell's instinct about the balance of nature had nothing specially English about it. It was a prefiguration of the universal humanism that is to be found in all his work.

History and literature, and their tradition and continuity, are often proposed as the cultural underlay of Englishness. But Orwell had nothing but contempt for the view of English history as a pageant of monarchs and a register of glorious battles. He never lost an opportunity, whether in his novels or his essays, to ridicule the '1066 And All That' school. He seems to have been pleased at the discovery that the great seventeenth-century 'Digger' pamphleteer, Gerrard

Winstanley, hailed originally from Wigan. Quoting at length
from a splendid piece of Winstanley's invective against the
Norman yoke, he ended the extract like this:

> Thou blindfold, drowsy England, that sleeps and
> snorts in the bed of covetousness, awake, awake!
> The enemy is upon thy back, he is ready to scale
> the walls and enter possession, and wilt not thou
> look out?
>
> If only our modern Trotskyists and Anarchists — who in
> effect are saying the same thing — could write prose like
> that!

Orwell in this regard was 'English' in the sense that Thomas
Rainsborough and Tom Paine were English: their ideas, too,
were intended for universal consumption. His favourite text
of justification was Milton's line: 'By the known rules of ancient liberty' — the English tradition that has had to be asserted against British authorities time and again.

At the very end, it is true, his feeling for violated nature
and defiled language welled up in a more 'traditional' form.
When Winston Smith is waiting in the frightening an-
techambers of the headquarters of the Thought Police, he
runs into Ampleforth, the frigid technician whose job it has
been to rewrite English literature nearer to the Party's desire.
How can such a diligent hack possibly have offended?

> 'It was an indiscretion, undoubtedly. We were producing
> a definitive edition of the poems of Kipling. I allowed the

word "God" to remain at the end of a line. I could not help it!' he added almost indignantly, raising his face to look at Winston. 'It was impossible to change the line. The rhyme was "rod" . . . Has it ever occurred to you,' he said, 'that the whole history of English poetry has been determined by the fact that the English language lacks rhymes?'

This Kipling moment, in the very bowels of the Ministry of Love, is preceded and succeeded by a dream which recurs to Winston. It is of a landscape which he privately calls 'the Golden Country':

It was an old, rabbit-bitten pasture, with a foot-track wandering across it and a molehill here and there. In the ragged hedge on the opposite side of the field the boughs of the elm trees were swaying very faintly in the breeze, their leaves just stirring in dense masses like women's hair. Somewhere near at hand, though out of sight, there was a clear, slow-moving stream where dace were swimming in the pools under the willow trees.

And from this dream 'Winston woke up with the word "Shakespeare" on his lips'. Whether this is the common land that Winstanley defended from the marauding nobles, or the more prettified and domesticated 'old, gold common' of A. A. Milne, it is undoubtedly not a corner of any foreign field.

6

Orwell and the Feminists
Difficulties with Girls

George Orwell's relationship with the female sex was in general a distraught one, and he had a tendency to let it show. We find the following in his last notebook; it is either the sketch of a short story or, more probably, an autobiographical fragment:

> The conversations he overheard as a small boy, between his mother, his aunt, his elder sister (?) & their feminist friends. The way in which, without ever hearing any direct statement to that effect, & without having more than a very dim idea of the relationship between the sexes, he derived a firm impression that women *did not like* men,

that they looked upon them as a sort of large, ugly, smelly & ridiculous animal, who maltreated women in every way, above all by forcing their attentions upon them. It was pressed deep into his consciousness, to remain there till he was abt 20, that sexual intercourse gives pleasure only to the man . . . & the picture of it in his mind was of a man pursuing a woman, forcing her down, & jumping on top of her, as he had often seen a cock do to a hen.

The narrator of *Keep the Aspidistra Flying* opens Chapter Six in the following way:

This woman business! What a bore it is! What a pity we can't cut it right out, or at least be like the animals — minutes of ferocious lust and months of icy chastity. Take a cock pheasant, for example. He jumps up on the hens' backs without so much as a with your leave or by your leave. And no sooner is it over than the whole subject is out of his mind. He hardly even notices his hens any longer; he ignores them, or simply pecks them if they come too near his food. He is not called upon to support his offspring, either. Lucky pheasant! How different from the lord of creation, always on the hop between his memory and his conscience!

Many a true word is spoken in jest and there is an obvious element of tongue-in-cheek in the above, but it's hardly an exaggeration to say that Orwell wrote for a male audience. Moreover, in neither his fiction nor his journalism is the word 'feminist' ever used except with, or as, a sneer. He included it in his famous taxonomy of weird and ludicrous beliefs, along with the fruit-juice drinkers, escaped Quakers, sandal-wearers and other cranks, in *The Road to Wigan Pier*. Thus, to the extent that there was a balance of power between the sexes, he seems to have felt that, if anything, it already favoured the female quite enough.

Biographers have not improved much upon his own writings in locating the source or sources of these woes. His mother was somewhat forbidding, perhaps (though less so than his father). He always felt himself unappetising to the opposite sex. At his infamous prep school, made imperishable in 'Such, Such Were the Joys', it was the headmaster's *wife*, the cruel and somehow knowing and devious 'Flip', who could find out his weak spots and subject him to humiliation. There is an especially powerful scene where this dreadful woman manages to combine the ignominy of bed-wetting, the threat of corporal punishment and the agony of sexual shame into one excruciating episode. The small Eric Blair was compelled to confront the idea of obscenity and indecency long before he had any concept of love or sex, let alone of the relation between the two.

Many young Englishmen, damaged in precisely that way, went off to the colonies and made themselves a nuisance to the 'native' women. Orwell never gave a reason for his sudden resignation from the Burma Police, but I am morally certain that it was this latent element, as well as a more generalized revulsion against imperialism, that caused him to make up his mind. The system of exploitation in Burma depended, in its social aspect, on a double indecency. Even the most educated Burmese or Indian man would and could be refused entry to

the English Club. But even the least educated Burmese girl
could be admitted to the white man's bungalow — for cash,
and via the back door. (Flory in *Burmese Days* admits, in a
little-noticed aside, to having actually *bought* his native mis-
tress from her family.) Moreover, in the repression of the
Burmese as a people there is an undeniable thrill of domination; it takes only a few phrases from the lips of Ellis, the club-
room sadist, to tell us what kind of filth is permanently flick-
ering in his mind, and how adept Orwell was at detecting it.

The latter point might be the crucial one, since insights
of that sort are more available to those who may have a guilty
share in them. Orwell could be tongue-in-cheek about this,
too, as when he wrote to his friend Brenda Salkeld in 1934:

> I had lunch yesterday with Mr Ede. He is a bit of a femi-
> nist and thinks that if a woman was brought up exactly
> like a man she would be able to throw a stone, construct a
> syllogism, keep a secret etc. He tells me that my antifemi-
> nist views are probably due to Sadism! I have never read
> the Marquis de Sade's novels — they are unfortunately
> very hard to get hold of.

Ms Salkeld was later to take the view, on the BBC Third Programme in 1960, that 'he didn't really like women'. This un-
falsifiable charge has been made since by a number of 'left'
feminists, most notably Beatrix Campbell in her 1984 book
Wigan Pier Revisited. The book is slightly encumbered by its
tendency to criticize Orwell for approaching matters from a
middle-class perspective, which of course was the whole
point of his expedition in the first place and is clearly stated

in the opening pages of the book. She is on somewhat surer turf when she reviews his masculine perspective, if only because that was not something he freely avowed at the start.

Alert to the ideological implications of the body and the gaze, Ms Campbell was quick to notice Orwell's emphasis on the physique of the coalminers; his discovery that: 'It is only when you see miners down the mine and naked that you realise what splendid men they are. Most of them are small (big men are at a disadvantage in that job) but nearly all of them have the most noble bodies; wide shoulders tapering to slender supple waists, and small pronounced buttocks and sinewy thighs, with not an ounce of waste flesh anywhere.' Certainly class is involved here — words like splendid and noble are applied by the officer corps to unusually good 'specimens' among the other ranks, and indeed Orwell found himself employing what Campbell describes as an Etonian accolade when he said that miners had figures 'fit for a guardsman'. (The National Union of Mineworkers was known until the mid 1980s as 'The Brigade of Guards of the Labour movement'.)

Is there a hint of the homoerotic here? It's difficult to argue confidently that there is not. We know that Orwell was teased heartlessly by Cyril Connolly while at Eton for being 'gone' on another boy and, while that might have been commonplace enough, we also have the claim by his friend and colleague Rayner Heppenstall that he was himself the object of an adult homosexual 'crush' on Orwell's part. The only really alluring girl in his fiction, the minx Elizabeth Lackersteen in *Burmese Days*, is depicted as extremely boyish in physique. Perhaps it isn't wise to press this too far, but the second-most alluring girl, Rosemary in *Keep the Aspidistra Flying*, is praised specifically for the charm of her 'behind'. Come to think of it, his second wife, Sonia Brownell, was known as 'Buttocks Brownell' even beyond the *louche* offices of *Horizon* magazine. But then, D. H. Lawrence evinced a certain interest in buttocks as well, and wrote tellingly about the beautiful bodies of coalminers, without coming in for the same suspicion of being closeted. I once asked Irving Kristol, who had helped Stephen Spender edit *Encounter* in the 1960s, how he had found the cultural translation from New York to the London of those days. He responded rather coldly that he and his wife had been astounded by how many homosexuals there seemed to be. I remember being shocked that he had been shocked. In the same way, it seems at least perverse of Orwell to have been surprised that, in the world of arts and letters, there should have been so many gentlemen who preferred gentlemen.

More suggestive in the pop-psychology sense is the very evident fact that Orwell seemed unable to stay off the subject. He went well out of his way to take a stick to 'nancy-boys', 'pansies' and 'sodomy' and this, as we have come to know, can be a bad sign. One isn't altogether sure, even so, that it licenses Ms Campbell's view that men are practitioners of 'mass narcissism' whereas women, 'because they are a subordinate sex', are not. For one thing, there seems to be a potential non sequitur here. Might narcissism not be a consolation to the subordinate?

The industrial areas visited by Orwell were dominated by cotton as well as coal, and Campbell rightly points out that by neglecting the former in favour of the latter in his researches, he overlooked the industrialization of female

labour. He overlooked it in the case of coal as well, being either unaware of or indifferent to the long history of women's
work 'on the pit brow'; this feminine contribution to coal-
heaving being quite specifically centred around Wigan.
Women are by no means invisible in Orwell's travelogue, but
they occur as wives or daughters or young persons caught in
domestic drudgery. If he had known of women working in
mining it seems likely that he would have been appalled;
most educated people imagined that women and children
had been spared such arduous work since at least the time of
Lord Shaftesbury.

At one point, Orwell intended to repeat his success in
deconstructing boys' weeklies with an essay on women's
magazines. Basing herself on the fragments of what he did
say, another feminist critic, Deirdre Beddoe, doesn't think
that this never-attempted or never-commissioned article
would have amounted to much:

> Orwell's awareness of class divisions in society went
> alongside his lack of understanding of gender divisions,
> and is summed up in his discussion of women's maga-
> zines. He was perceptively aware that these magazines
> project a fantasy of 'pretending to be richer than you are'
> for the bored factory-girl or worn-out mother of five, but
> totally unaware of how these magazines reinforced gender
> divisions in society and promoted the dominant female
> stereotype of the interwar years — the housewife.

This might be a sin of omission. Ms Beddoe goes on to complain of the women in Orwell's novels, who are either shrews

or geese, vamps or frumps, or else (Julia in *Nineteen Eighty-Four* excepted) grasping and conformist. This, as it happens, is true. It is even true of Mollie, 'the foolish, pretty white mare' of *Animal Farm*, who sells herself out for a handful of ribbons and a couple of sugarlumps. Not that the men in these novels — moth-eaten, either scrawny or bloated, selfish, resentful and repressed — are exactly paragons. However, Ms Beddoe is right about one thing. Every one of the female characters is practically devoid of the least trace of intellectual or reflective capacity. Elizabeth Lackersteen is mindlessly low-brow to an extent that shocks even the besotted Flory when he discerns it. Dorothy in *A Clergyman's Daughter* operates on blind and simple Christian faith, can't keep her end up in an elementary argument with the village atheist, and collapses at the same time as her beliefs. George Bowling's wife Hilda, in *Coming Up for Air*, is a tight-fisted and joyless type who only comes with him to meetings of the Left Book Club because admittance is free. The sweet-natured Rosemary in *Keep the Aspidistra Flying* never even pretends to have the smallest idea what Gordon is talking about. When Winston Smith begins to read the excitingly dangerous forbidden manuscript of Emmanuel Goldstein aloud in *Nineteen Eighty-Four*, his supposed co-conspirator Julia promptly falls fast asleep.

What can be said in Orwell's defence here? Part of his novelistic enterprise was to represent the dead-endishness of much English life. Few images can emphasize this more tellingly than that of a woman wasting away. In one of the best passages of *A Clergyman's Daughter*, Dorothy finds herself trapped as a teacher in a hideous school whose precise purpose is the deliberate stultification of young girls. George

Bowling recoils from the sight of a female shop-assistant being bullied and tormented by a nasty male overseer. Though Campbell and Beddoe don't notice it, accusing him of ignoring the vast submerged workforce of female domestic servants, his novels and columns make frequent reference to the abysmal existence led by precisely this 'skivvy' class. And when Beddoe says, of *Keep the Aspidistra Flying*, that it shows stupid female readers infatuated with tenth-rate women authors, but not the male equivalent of either reader or author, she merely convicts herself of not having finished what is, after all, a fairly short and straightforward novel.

In his time, we know that Orwell married one very tough-minded and intelligent woman, Eileen O'Shaughnessy, whose life was lost to a botched hospital operation. He later admitted to having treated her poorly on occasion, but all witnesses are agreed that he was devoted to her and was made almost wordless by her death. He fell in love with Celia Kirwan, one of the most brilliant as well as one of the most beautiful of her generation, and proposed marriage to her without success. In his near-death agony he proposed successfully to Sonia Brownell who, difficult as she was, could not be described as shallow or vapid. This deserves to be entered on the credit side of the account even if, as we have lately learned, the dying Orwell sometimes suggested to women that they might be tempted by the lifetime sinecure of 'writer's widow'. Even with its indignity and pathos, this is not an offer he would have made to anyone he suspected of being mindless.

'Women in Orwell's fiction,' observes Beddoe rather tritely, 'are not capable of happiness without men.' It would be equally acute to say that they — Dorothy for instance — are incapable of happiness, or are made unhappy by men. And it would certainly be true to say that men in Orwell's fiction are utterly incapable of happiness without women. Yes, they resent the need of women, as many men do, and as Orwell himself obviously did. Yes, they distrust the marriage bond as a 'trap' set by a hypocritical and acquisitive society. But to write about male–female relations in any decade and to omit these elements would have been to abandon verisimilitude.

Viewed with discrimination, Orwell's actual prejudice turns out to be against the sexless woman, or the woman who has lost her sex and become shrivelled and/or mannish. This is an old male trope; it appears to conform in his case with a wider dislike or suspicion of anything 'unnatural'. The big surprise, in reviewing feminist criticism of him, is the failure to notice his revulsion for birth control and abortion. He never treated either subject to a full-length review, but shied away with disgust whenever it was forced on his attention. During the Second World War, he noticed that goods requiring scarce rubber had become shoddy and hard to find, whereas male contraceptives were of good quality and easy to come by. Whenever he did a word-portrait of a future mindless caretaker state, the list of its sub-Utopian features was certain to include a contemptuous reference to a birth control clinic or an abortion centre. And whenever he wrote about population, he took the gloomily anti-Malthusian view that it was failing to reproduce itself with enough speed or vigour. It does seem from certain letters and memoirs that he believed himself to be sterile; this added to the larger burden under which he toiled in his relations with women.

Rosemary in *Keep the Aspidistra Flying* is the grand exception here. Even when pregnant as a result of her very first (and very disappointing) sexual encounter, she refuses to employ any moral blackmail against the unlovable Gordon Comstock. It is therefore on his own initiative that he decides to consider the responsibility of choosing between the sin of abortion and the 'trap' of marriage, one of the oldest dilemmas in modern fiction. We know Comstock's silly and self-pitying voice well enough by this stage, so it is fairly obviously Orwell speaking when a suddenly mature Gordon has his epiphany:

> For the first time he grasped, *with the only kind of knowledge that matters*, what they were really talking about. The words 'a baby' took on a new significance. They did not mean any longer a mere abstract disaster, they meant a bud of flesh, a bit of himself, down there in her belly, alive and growing. His eyes met hers. They had a strange moment of sympathy such as they had never had before. For a moment he did feel that in some mysterious way they were one flesh. Though they were feet apart he felt as though they were joined together — as though some invisible living cord stretched from her entrails to his. He knew then that it was a dreadful thing they were contemplating — blasphemy, if that word had any meaning [my italics].

One could hardly wish, in a few sentences, for a clearer proof of the way in which Orwell relied upon the instinctual. The impalpable umbilicus unites the couple as well as the mother and child; to sever it prematurely, for any selfish motive, is to commit an un-nameable but none the less intelligible offence against humanity.

Of course, no sooner does Gordon go to the public library to consult some volumes on embryology and pregnancy than he is confronted by another foe: 'The woman at the desk was a university graduate, young, colourless, spectacled, and intensely disagreeable . . . Gordon knew her type at a glance . . . '

There are limits to plain old decency and common sense, we may be sure. Orwell was the cause of a domestic dispute in one of the Yorkshire slum homes in which he lodged, as a consequence of doing what any well-bred middle-class guest would do, and helping Mrs Searle with the washing-up. Her husband and another male guest were very much put out. Mrs Searle herself remained neutral in the dispute. And Orwell noticed that it was the women quite as much as the men who expected domestic chores to be performed on the distaff side: 'I believe that they, as well as the men, feel that a man would lose his manhood if, merely because he was out of work, he developed into a "Mary Ann".' He also wrote that this distinguished the proletarian home from the middle-class one, where the boss of the house was quite likely to be the woman, or even the baby. Taking this as her starting point, Janet Montefiore interrogates Orwell's subjectivity about females. Her book *Men and Women Writers of the 1930s: The Dangerous Flood of History* is by some distance the most acute feminist reading of the period. However, she employs a somewhat standard vocabulary in approaching Orwell's well-known narration of the wretched young woman glimpsed from the relatively lordly perspective of a passing train:

> Orwell's documentary image of the inarticulate slum girl whose sordid physical suffering represents the general misery of the working class, use[s] the image of a woman's body as a class signifier . . . The rhetorical trope whereby a woman's body personifies a class is a common feature of the Socialist writings of the thirties — far more so, in fact, than the maternal harpies in the plays of Auden, Isherwood and Spender, which have few parallels elsewhere.

True enough, but the vision of a young girl deprived of her prime and reduced to drudgery and shame is a 'trope' which one would not have wished, as a campaigner against needless poverty and ignorance, to be without. And had Orwell omitted this figure, and others like her, there would certainly have been other feminists to say that he rendered the female form 'invisible'. Ms Montefiore seems to both admit and discount this possibility when she writes later that: 'Orwell's slum girl is seen to suffer with complete consciousness of her "dreadful destiny", even if her dumb awareness can only be articulated by the bourgeois male writer's eye and mind.' This kind of diagnosed 'objectification' necessarily flirts with tautology: we would not have seen this woman if Orwell had not been struck by witnessing her extremity; it is he who decides from the look on her face that she is not suffering like an animal but is somehow alive to the gruesomeness of her condition. Is he not, rather, articulating her articulation? Thus, for

Montefiore to write that 'the way in which women's physical misery is turned into a metonym for class suffering implies some powerful specifically bourgeois fantasies about gendered bodies and knowledge' is to make a highly unverifiable claim. The alternative, she suggests, is to *be* that woman yourself, to undergo the 'experience of concrete particulars: the sweaty and aching body, the finger exploring grime'. This would be not so much abandoning the subjective as actually becoming the subject — an impossible demand under any circumstances and one that flatly negates the purpose of realistic, first-hand narrative writing.

One conclusion might be that Orwell liked and desired the *feminine* but was somewhat put on his guard by the *female*. And he really didn't like, and may even have feared, either feminine men or masculine women. With a reserved part of himself, he suspected that the war between the sexes was an unalterable feature of the natural order. In his better moments, he did not give credit to the natural order for such things as the sexual division of labour, or the tyranny of domestic relations. Victim of a narrow-minded patriarch himself, he would have liked to be a firm but gentle father. But benevolent patriarchy is, quite rightly, the very assumption that feminism exists to challenge. We are still witnesses to, and participants in, the battle over what is and what is not, in human and sexual relations, 'natural'. At least it can be said for Orwell that he registered his participation in this unending conflict with a decent minimum of hypocrisy.

7

'The List'

It was easy enough for me to say, in an earlier chapter, that Orwell was essentially 'right' about the three great issues of fascism, Stalinism and Empire, and that he was enabled to be 'right' by a certain insistence on intellectual integrity and independence. The question arises, was it possible for him to uphold all these positions, and in that way, simultaneously?

I choose a representative quotation from Paul Lashmar and James Oliver's book, *Britain's Secret Propaganda War*, a history of the 'Information Research Department' (IRD) of the British Foreign Office:

> George Orwell's reputation as a left-wing icon took a body-blow from which it may never recover when it was revealed in 1996 that he had cooperated closely with

IRD's Cold Warriors, even offering his own blacklist of eighty-six Communist 'fellow-travellers'. As the *Daily Telegraph* noted, 'To some, it was as if Winston Smith had willingly cooperated with the Thought Police in *1984*.'

This, or something like it, is a recounting of events that now enjoys quite extensive currency. It is easy to demonstrate, if only by the supporting evidence presented by Lashmar and Oliver, that it is wholly mistaken. And I have selected their synopsis because it is free of the Orwell-hatred that disfigures many other versions of the story.

Just as a matter of record, then:

1. The existence of Orwell's list of Stalinized intellectuals was not 'revealed' in 1996. It appears in Professor Bernard Crick's biography, which was first published in 1980.

2. A blacklist is a roster of names maintained by those with the power to affect hiring and firing. To be blacklisted is to be denied employment for political reasons unconnected to job-performance. The word does not now, and never has had, any other meaning.

3. Even if the *Daily Telegraph* says so, and even if it has chosen not to specify the 'some' who chose to think it, the Information Research Department was unconnected to any 'Thought Police', to say nothing of the Thought Police as they actually feature in the pages of *Nineteen Eighty-Four*.

But this is by no means to exhaust the utter distortion of
Orwell's motives and methods that is involved in the rapid
but shallow dissemination of this 'disclosure'. The simple
facts of the case are these. Together with his friend Richard
Rees, Orwell had for some time enjoyed playing what Rees
himself called a 'parlour game'. This game consisted of guess-
ing which public figures would, or would not, sell out in the
event of an invasion or a dictatorship. Orwell had been playing this game, in a serious as well as a frivolous way, for years.
On New Year's Day 1942 he wrote, in a lengthy despatch for
Partisan Review, about the varieties of defeatist opinion to be
found among British journalists and intellectuals. His tone
was detached; he noted the odd alliances between widely discrepant factions. He also analysed the temptation among intellectuals to adapt themselves to power, as instanced by developments across the Channel:

> Both Vichy and the Germans have found it quite easy to
> keep a facade of 'French culture' in existence. Plenty of
> intellectuals were ready to go over, and the Germans were
> quite ready to make use of them, even when they were
> 'decadent.' At this moment Drieu de la Rochelle is editing
> the *Nouvelle Revue Française*, Pound is bellowing against
> the Jews on the Rome radio, and Céline is a valued ex-
> hibit in Paris, or at least his books are. All of these would
> come under the heading of *kulturbolschewismus*, but they
> are also useful cards to play against the intelligentsia in
> Britain and the U.S.A. If the Germans got to England,

similar things would happen, *and I think I could make out
at least a preliminary list of the people who would go over*
[my italics].

Notice the date of this. It should be borne in mind here that
until recently the Soviet Union had been in a military alliance with Hitler — an alliance loudly defended by Britain's
Communists — and that Moscow Radio had denounced the
British naval blockade of Nazi Germany as a barbaric war on
civilians. The German Communist Party had published a
statement in 1940 in which it was discovered that for dialec-
tical reasons the British empire was somewhat worse than the
National Socialist one. Orwell never tired of pointing these
things out; they were the sort of illusions or delusions that
could have real consequences. Nor did he omit to mention
and specify the sorts of intellectual — E. H. Carr being a celebrated instance — who could transfer their allegiance with
sinister smoothness from one despotic regime to another.

No less to the point, he had discovered in Spain that the
Communist strategy relied very heavily upon the horror and
terror of anonymous denunciation, secret informing, and police espionage. At that date, the official hero of all young Communists was Pavlik Morozov, a 14-year old 'Pioneer' who had
turned in his family to the Soviet police for the offence of
hoarding grain. The villagers had slain him as a result; statues
of the martyr-child were commonplace in the USSR and it was
the obligation of a good Party member to emulate his example.

Orwell's disgust at this culture of betrayal was not confined
to the visceral style by which he portrayed and condemned it

in *Nineteen Eighty-Four*. He showed a lifelong hatred for all forms of censorship, proscription and blacklisting. Even when Sir Oswald Mosley was released from prison at the height of the Second World War — a piece of lenience which inspired many complaints from supposed anti-fascists — Orwell commented that it was unpleasant to see the Left protesting at the application of habeas corpus. He took the same line with those who objected to lifting the government ban on the publication of the *Daily Worker*, only taking time to notice that this habit of intolerance had been acquired by many people from the *Daily Worker's* own editors. In May 1946 he wrote that the main danger from any Communist-led split in the Labour movement was that it 'could hardly result in a Communist-controlled government, but it might bring back the Conservatives — which, I suppose, would be less dangerous from the Russian point of view than the spectacle of a Labour government making a success of things'.

This last sentence approaches the crux of the matter. The extreme Left and the democratic Left had concluded in different ways that Stalinism was a negation of socialism and not a version of it. Orwell had seen the extreme Left massacred by Stalin's agents in Spain, and he was one of the few to call attention to the execution of the Social Democrats Ehrlich and Alter in Stalinized Poland. For him, the quarrel with the 'Stalintern' was not an academic question, or a difference of degree. He felt it as an intimate and very present threat. And the campaign to ban or restrict his books — to 'blacklist' him and his writings — had been led by surreptitious Communist sympathizers who worked both in publishing and in the offices of the

British state. It was a bureaucrat in the Ministry of Information named Peter Smolka who had quietly helped orchestrate the near-suppression of *Animal Farm*. One might therefore put it like this: in the late 1940s Orwell was fighting for survival as a writer, and also considered the survival of democratic and socialist values to be at stake in the struggle against Stalin.

Was it possible to conduct this struggle without lending oneself to 'the forces of reaction'? In everything he wrote and did at the time, Orwell strove to make exactly that distinction. He helped to organize and circulate a statement from the Freedom Defence Committee which objected to the purge of supposed political extremists from the Civil Service, insisting that secret vetting procedures be abolished and that the following safeguards be implemented:

A. The individual whose record is being investigated should be permitted to call a trade union or other representative to speak on his behalf.

B. All allegations should be required to be substantiated by corroborative evidence, this being particularly essential in the case of allegations made by representatives of MI5 or the Special Branch of Scotland Yard, when the sources of information are not revealed.

C. The Civil Servant concerned, or his representative, should be allowed to cross-examine those giving evidence against him.

Signed by, among others, Orwell, E. M. Forster, Osbert Sitwell and Henry Moore, this statement was first published in the *Socialist Leader* on 21 August 1948. (I cannot resist noting that this was twenty years to the day before the Soviet occupation of Czechoslovakia, and saw print at the time when Czechoslovakia was being efficiently Stalinized, as well as ethnically cleansed of its German-speaking inhabitants, with the collaboration of many apparently 'non-Party' front organizations. Orwell was one of the few to inveigh against either development, anticipating both Ernest Gellner and Václav Havel by seeing the anti-German racism as a demagogic cover for an authoritarian and nationalist state.) These details do not appear in any published work on the subject of Orwell's supposed role as a police spy; most accounts preferring to draw back in shock at the very idea of any contact with the British Foreign Office.

What, then, was the extent of this contact? On 29 March 1949 Orwell received a visit at his hospital bedside from Celia Kirwan, who was among other things an official of the IRD. She was also the sister-in-law of Arthur Koestler, and Orwell had already, in that capacity, met her and proposed marriage to her. They discussed the necessity of recruiting socialist and radical individuals to the fight against the Communists. This subject was already close to Orwell's heart, as can be seen from the story of his effort to get *Animal Farm* circulated clandestinely in Eastern Europe (see pp. 90–91). Ms Kirwan was close to his heart also, and some defenders of Orwell have kindly suggested that this, together with his much-etiolated physical condition, may have led to a moment of weakness. I find this defence both sentimental and improbable. He told her what he would have told anyone, and what he said in print whenever the opportunity afforded itself, which was that many presentable leftists of good reputation were not to be trusted when it came to the seductions of Moscow. On 6 April he wrote to Richard Rees asking him to find and forward his 'quarto notebook with a pale-bluish cardboard cover', in which could be found 'a list of crypto-Communists & fellow-travellers which I want to bring up to date'. This in itself shows that Orwell had not originally drawn up the list at the behest of the state. No doubt there was another notebook with the names of the old Nazi sympathizers and potential collaborators, but no matter. Orwell is not today being impeached for keeping lists, merely for keeping them on the wrong people.

The incurable inanity of British officialdom and 'official secrecy' means that the list of 35 names given to Celia Kirwan is still not open to our scrutiny. The Public Record Office states demurely and fatuously that 'a document has been withheld by the Foreign Office'. It was at one point conceivable that this measure was taken to protect living people from Orwell's posthumous opinion; even that absurd pretext must now have decayed with time. However, we have the notebook if not the 'update' and we do not require official permission to make up our own minds.

The list certainly illustrates Orwell's private resentments and eccentricities. Very little of it, in point of fact, materializes Rees's confirmation that 'this was a sort of game we played — discussing who was a paid agent of what and estimating to what lengths of treachery our favourite *bêtes noires* would be prepared to go'. To be exact, only one person is ever accused of being an agent, and even there the qualifying words 'almost certainly' are applied. This was Peter Smolka, alias Smollett, a former Beaverbook newspaper executive and holder of the OBE, who was the very official in the Ministry of Information who had put pressure on Jonathan Cape to drop *Animal Farm*. It has since been conclusively established that Smolka was indeed an agent of Soviet security; this represents a match of 100 per cent between Orwell's allegation of direct foreign recruitment and the known facts. As he phrased it rather mildly in his letter to Celia Kirwan, enclosing his list that wasn't 'very sensational and I don't suppose it will tell your friends anything they don't know . . . If it had been done earlier it would have stopped people like Peter Smollett worming their way into important propaganda jobs where they were probably able to do us a lot of harm.' The 'us' here is the democratic Left. On the very same day, Orwell wrote to Richard Rees, saying that just because a certain Labour MP was a friend of the flagrant and notorious Konni Zilliacus, this did not prove he was 'a crypto'. He added: 'It seems to me very important to attempt to gauge people's *subjective* feelings, because otherwise one can't predict their behaviour in situations where the results of certain actions are clear even to a self-deceiver . . . The whole difficulty is to decide where each person stands, & one has to treat each case individually.' The staffers of Senator Joseph McCarthy did not possess even the inklings of this discrimination.

Few of the thumbnail sketches run to more than a dozen or so freehand and laconic words. And many of them stand the test of time remarkably well. Who could object to the summary of Kingsley Martin as 'Decayed liberal. Very dishonest'? Or, to take another and later editor of the *New Statesman*, to the shrewd characterization of Richard Crossman as '??Political climber. Zionist (appears sincere about this.) Too dishonest to be outright F. T. [fellow-traveller]'? The latter has a nice paradox to it; Orwell had a respect for honest Leninists. Almost one-third of the entries end in the verdict 'Probably not', or 'Sympathiser only', in the space reserved for Party allegiance. J. B. Priestley is recorded as making huge sums from advantageously published Soviet editions of his works; well, so he did, as it now turns out.

Some critics, notably Frances Stonor Saunders in her book *Who Paid The Piper?*, have allowed a delicate wrinkling of the nostril at Orwell's inclusion of details about race, and what is now termed 'sexual preference'. It is true that Isaac Deutscher is listed as a 'Polish Jew', and it is also true that he was a Polish Jew. But then Louis Adamic is identified — and why not? — as 'Born in Slovenia not Croatia'. The protean Konni Zilliacus, then a very influential figure, is queried rather than identified as 'Finnish? "Jewish"?' (He was both.) I have to admit that I laughed out loud at seeing Stephen Spender described as having a 'Tendency to homosexuality', which would not precisely define him, and at seeing Tom Driberg written down as merely 'Homosexual', which was not to say the half of it. Ms Saunders comments haughtily that accusations of that kind could get a chap into trouble in those days. Well, not in the British Secret Service or Foreign Office, they couldn't, as Guy Burgess could have assured her. Hugh McDiarmid, the Stalin-worshipping Scots poet, was described by Orwell as 'Very anti-English'. My friend Perry Anderson, editor of the *New Left Review*, made something of this too, until I pointed out that McDiarmid had listed 'Anglophobia' as one of his recreations in *Who's Who*. And it was Perry Anderson who published, in his 'Components of the National Culture' in *New Left Review* in 1968, a chart giving the ethnic and national origins of the Cold War émigré intellectuals in Britain, from Namier, Berlin, Gombrich and Malinowski to Popper, Melanie Klein and indeed Isaac Deutscher. He reprinted the diagram in his book *English Questions* in 1992. I defended him both times. These things about people are worth knowing.

There are some crankish bits in the list, as when Paul Robeson is written off as 'Very anti-white'. But even some of the more tentative judgements about Americans are otherwise quite perceptive. Henry Wallace, as editor of the *New Republic*, had already caused Orwell to cease sending contributions to a magazine in which he could sense a general softness on Stalin. In 1948, Wallace's campaign for the American presidency probably ruined and compromised the American Left for a generation, because of his reliance on Communist Party endorsement and organization. Veteran leftist critics of the Truman administration, notably I. F. Stone, were mentally and morally tough enough to point this out at the time.

All too much has been made of this relatively trivial episode, the last chance for Orwell's enemies to vilify him for being correct. The points to keep one's eye on are these: the IRD was not interested or involved in domestic surveillance, and wanted only to recruit staunch socialists and Social

Democrats; nobody suffered or could have suffered from Orwell's private opinion; he said nothing in 'private' that he did not consistently say in public. And, while a few on 'the list' were known personally to Orwell, most were not. This has its importance, since a 'snitch' or stool pigeon is rightly defined as someone who betrays friends or colleagues in the hope of plea-bargaining, or otherwise of gaining advantage, for himself. By no imaginable stretch could Orwell's views of Congressman Claud Pepper, or of Vice-President Wallace, fall into this category. Nor could it (or did it) damage their careers. And there is no entry on 'the list' that comes anywhere near, for sheer sulphuric contempt, Orwell's published challenge to Professor J. D. Bernal, and the other editors of the *Modern Quarterly*, to come clean about whether they were conscious agents of Stalin or not. In May 1946, in the pages of the short-lived *Polemic*, he asked:

> What exactly does Professor Bernal mean by 'fellowship' and 'ever-closer understanding' between Britain and the USSR? Does he mean, for instance, that independent British observers in large numbers should be allowed to travel freely through Soviet territory and send home uncensored reports? Or that Soviet citizens should be encouraged to read British newspapers, listen to the BBC and view the institutions of this country with a friendly eye? Obviously he doesn't mean that. All he can mean, therefore, is that Russian propaganda in this country should be intensified, and that critics of the Soviet regime

(darkly referred to as 'subtle disseminators of mutual suspicion') should be silenced.*

Let us take the case of Konni Zilliacus, now forgotten but
even in my lifetime a leading figure of the Labour Left. Orwell accused him in *Tribune* of being a willing deputy of the
Soviet design, and the two men had quite a barbed exchange
as a consequence. It ended like this. In 1946 Orwell and others publicly asked Zilliacus to confirm or deny that he had
referred to Communist Poland and East Germany as genuine democracies. Zilliacus replied:

> What I actually said in both the Soviet zone of Germany
> and Poland was that what I had seen was not parliamen-
> tary democracy as we knew it in the West, which was the
> most mature and highly developed form of democracy,
> but revolutionary democracy, democracy in the primitive
> and original sense of Abraham Lincoln's great definition of
> 'government of the people, by the people, for the people.'

---

*As late as his *Two Cultures* lectures in the mid 1960s, C. P. Snow could dare to
say that:

> If the scientists have the future in their bones, then the traditional culture
> responds by wishing the future did not exist . . . Compare George Orwell's
> *Nineteen Eighty-Four*, which is the strongest possible wish that the future
> should not exist, with J. D. Bernal's *World Without War.*

This slander on Orwell, and this fawning on Stalin's most prominent 'scientific'
fan, was well received in the academy, not just after the Lysenko scandal but after
the revelations of the Khrushchev 'secret speech' of 1956.

This reads today as it read then — as a condemnation of Zilliacus out of his own mouth. But what is not appreciated today is the relative strength of similar opinions among intellectuals and academics and trade unionists at the time. It was against that pervasive mentality that Orwell was contending. Let it be noticed, however, that he didn't approve at all of the British intervention in Greece (the undeclared clause in the Churchill–Stalin pact over Poland) and that he even, with misgivings, signed a petition to reduce the sentence of Alan Nunn-May, a scientist who had handed nuclear formulae — it would be a stretch to call them 'secrets', as Orwell appreciated — to the Soviet Union.

One can also eliminate the mercenary motive. Some of those who worked with the IRD were later paid, modestly enough it is true, to write pamphlets or booklets showing that Stalin or Mao were not just enthusiastic land-reformers. Later in its life, the IRD went the way of many British Cold-War outfits and surrendered to the lavish corruption of the CIA. However, Orwell continued to make no money for his publications, to refuse to charge exile groups any royalties, and in general to act as if the ravens would feed him. The subsequent largesse with which magazines like *Encounter* were floated was enough to arouse the suspicion and contempt of people much more avaricious than he was. It must therefore be very much doubted that he would have approved, in a more exorbitant and cynical time, of the sorts of tactic that he had eschewed even in the age of austerity.

This was the period during which Orwell's samizdat editions of *Animal Farm* were being confiscated in Germany by

American officers and either burned on the spot or turned
over to the Red Army. It was indeed difficult for him to oppose Stalinism and Western imperialism at the same time,
while attempting to hold on to his independence. But the
stupidity of the state only helped to make certain that, at any
rate while he lived, he was always its victim and never its servant. The British Foreign Office, which had been erring on
Stalin's side for almost a decade, suddenly needed anti-
Stalinist energy in the mid 1940s. It had nowhere to turn, in
its search for credible and honest writers, but to the *Tribune*
Left. This is not, taking the medium or the long view of history, the most disgraceful moment in the record of British socialism. It is also part of the reason why there was no
McCarthyite panic or purge in Britain. The *trahison des clercs*
was steadily opposed, in both its Stalinoid and its conservative form, by groups like the Freedom Defence Committee.
Orwell cannot posthumously be denied his credit for keeping
that libertarian and honest tradition alive. The Cold War involved many things, including a vertiginously dangerous
arms race, an attempt to keep colonialism on a life-support
system, an unguessed-at level of suborning (or persecuting
and intimidating) of public intellectuals, and even some overt
collusion with former pro-Nazi elements in Eastern and Central Europe. But it also involved a confrontation with the poi-
sonous illusion that the Soviet system had a claim on the
democratic Left. In this essential confrontation, Orwell kept
his little corner of the Cold War fairly clean.

8

Generosity and Anger
The Novels

The waiter retired and came back with a folded slip on a
salver. Gordon opened it. Six and threepence — and he
had exactly seven and elevenpence in the world! Of course
he had known approximately what the bill must be, and
yet it was a shock now that it came. He stood up, felt in
his pocket and took out all his money. The sallow young
waiter, his salver on his arm, eyed the handful of money;
plainly he divined that it was all Gordon had. Rosemary
also had got up and come around the table. She pinched
Gordon's elbow; this was a signal that she would like to
pay her share. Gordon pretended not to notice. He paid
the six and threepence, and, as he turned away, dropped
another shilling onto the salver. The waiter balanced it for
a moment on his hand, flicked it over, and then slipped it
into his waistcoat pocket with the air of covering up something unmentionable.

✍ GEORGE ORWELL: *Keep the Aspidistra Flying*

A youthful waiter had approached . . . Dixon thought
he'd never seen a human frame radiating so much inso-
lence without recourse to speech, gesture, or any contor-
tion of the features . . . 'Four shillings,' the waiter said at
Dixon's side. His voice, heard now for the first time, suggested that he had a half-eaten sweet at the back of his
throat. Dixon searched his pockets and gave him two
half-crowns.

    ✑ KINGSLEY AMIS: *Lucky Jim*

In his lifetime, Orwell never ceased to apologize for his shortcomings as a writer of fiction. And at his death, he directed his
executors to ensure that at least two of his novels — *A Clergyman's Daughter* and *Keep the Aspidistra Flying* — were not re-
published. Overcome with a certain arch self-deprecation in
the course of composing 'Writers and Leviathan', he blamed
the times in which he lived for his failure to become a serious
literary contributor, instead of 'a sort of pamphleteer'. Staying
with the untidy formulation 'sort of ', he added:

> We have developed a sort of compunction which our
> grandparents did not have, an awareness of the enormous
> injustice and misery of the world, and a guilt-stricken
> feeling that one ought to be doing something about it,
> which makes a purely aesthetic attitude towards life im-
> possible. No one, now, could devote himself to literature
> as single-mindedly as Joyce or Henry James.

Though this belongs to Orwell's mature period, it is curiously adolescent in tone. (*Finnegans Wake* was completed in 1939, after all, and were not George Eliot and Thomas Hardy, to say nothing of Dostoyevsky, alive to injustice and misery?) At one point, he announced that he had destroyed the manuscripts of two novels written in his down-and-out Parisian days, an unverifiable claim that has the reek of the garret about it. Much later, he announced to friends that he had in mind a grand novel-sequence, of the 'family saga' kind, of which only a few notebook jottings survive. Clearly, he was insecure when it came to the fictional plunge.

He was, as we have seen, no great subscriber to the Leavis school. Yet he might have found little to disagree with in the verdict of Q. D. Leavis in *Scrutiny* of September 1940. Occupied only with Orwell's four pre-war novels, this notice began with a dose of the usual Leavisite provincial and Puritan malice:

> Mr Orwell . . . belongs by birth and education to the 'right Left people,' the nucleus of the literary world who christian-name each other and are in honour bound to advance each other's literary career; he figures indeed in Connolly's autobiography as a schoolfellow. This is probably why he has received indulgent treatment in the literary press.

Nothing could have been more calculated to annoy Orwell, who had produced quasi-Leavisite invective of his own against the spoiled little salons of the London literary elite.

However, a note of lenience and condescension on Mrs
Leavis's part was then permitted to be heard:

> He differs from them in having grown up . . . Starting
> from an inside knowledge of the working-class, painfully
> acquired, he can see through the Marxist theory, and be-
> ing innately decent (he displays and approves of bour-
> geois morality) he is disgusted with the callous theorising
> inhumanity of the pro-Marxists . . . Mr. Orwell must
> have wasted a lot of energy trying to be a novelist — I
> think I must have read three or four novels by him, and
> the only impression these dreary books left on me is that
> nature didn't intend him to be a novelist. *Yet his equiva-*
> *lent works in non-fiction are stimulating* [my italics].

It's touching to see Mrs Leavis partly anticipating a point
later made by Lionel Trilling — that Orwell treasured certain
'bourgeois' values because he thought they might come in
handy as revolutionary ones. However, the novels do carry
on a certain stubborn if stunted existence, if only because
they act as precursors to *Animal Farm* and *Nineteen Eighty-
Four*, and they are evidence in themselves of Orwell's determination to take the risk of fiction at almost any cost.

The themes of 'injustice and misery' are certainly not absent. It might be more accurate to say, however, that their
common subject is what Erich Fromm in another context
called 'the struggle against pointlessness'. The squalor and
deprivation take second and even third place to an oppressive
sense of futility and even of despair. And they were of course

written, in point of time as well as in point of Orwell's own life, in a context of poverty and ugliness and austerity, as well as a context in which the knell-like words 'the war' might be a reference to the next one as well as the last one.

In their limited place, however, these novels can now be seen as the forerunners to the tiresomely named 'Angry Young Man' literary productions of the 1950s, and also to the existentialist and absurdist works of that period, as well as to the gritty 'Northern' school of social realism which found its way into early British cinema as well as onto the London stage. Gordon Comstock in *Keep The Aspidistra Flying* and Jim Dixon in *Lucky Jim* (a novel published in 1954 and incidentally dedicated to the then obscure Philip Larkin) have more in common than their humiliations at the hands of jumped-up waiters, inflicted upon them while they are trying their impoverished best to impress charming young women. They both live in furnished lodgings of farcical gloom with the occasional highly 'difficult' or eccentric fellow-lodger. They are both weighed down with worthless pieces of 'work in progress'. They both measure out their lives in cigarettes, nervously calculating whether the next one was really reserved for the following day, or sometimes the following week. They are both put upon by pompous and condescending elders. They both resort to hideous excess of alcohol if the chance presents itself, and each registers a startling 'morning after' description. They both have a hard time with girls, at least partly due to lack of privacy and lack of funds. They both have a rich patron who acts as deus ex machina. They both find the English establishment to be essentially a transparent racket got up by the undeserving rich. (Amazingly, the prettiest girl in Jim Dixon's sorely neglected class is named Eileen O'Shaughnessy, the name of Orwell's first wife. Amis himself was later to have a brief fling with Sonia Brownell, Orwell's second wife and official widow.)

The tone of the two novels is, however, as different as could be imagined. Jim Dixon is only intermittently self-pitying and his life is threadbare rather than sordid. His attitude towards women is both more trusting and more grateful. His England, furthermore, is not a place of unrelieved dankness and conformity; the hints of post-war affluence and opportunity are everywhere, and shoots of hope keep obtruding themselves: nice things as opposed to nasty things, as Jim tells himself with conviction. He is, it could be argued, living in a time after the depression and the war, when the organized pressure of reformism has to some extent drawn the fangs of the class system. He is even able to assert himself, to rebel:

> [He] came back again and approached the waiter, who was leaning against the wall. 'Can I have my change, please?'
> 'Change?'
> 'Yes, change. Can I have it please?'
> 'Five shillings you give me.'
> 'Yes. The bill was four shillings. I want a shilling back.' . . . The waiter made no attempt to produce any money. In his half-choked voice he said:
> 'Most people give me a tip.'
> 'Most people would have kicked your arse for you by now.'

While the closest that Gordon comes to any version of resistance or optimism occurs to him as an unwelcome paradox while he is attempting to become a perfect drop-out: 'The strange thing is that often it is harder to sink than to rise. There is always something that drags one upwards.'

The opening pages of Kingsley Amis's *That Uncertain Feeling* discover a shabbily dressed John Lewis dealing with moronic or affected clients at a provincial public library. The evocation of Gordon Comstock's stifling routine at the lending section of the Hampstead bookstore is almost immediate, but again Amis's insistent humour and sexual subversiveness can't help dragging things upwards.

It was Orwell who famously adapted G. K. Chesterton's characterization of the 'Good Bad Book' in an essay published in 1945. His own rather lame definition — 'the kind of book that has no literary pretensions but which remains readable when more serious productions have perished' — was applied to the worlds of Sherlock Holmes and Uncle Tom. Harriet Beecher Stowe's popular classic he described as 'an unintentionally ludicrous book, full of preposterous melodramatic incidents; it is also deeply moving and essentially true; it is hard to say which quality outweighs the other'. Towards the end of his life Orwell wrote to Anthony Powell in near-despair over the hash he had made of *Nineteen Eighty-Four*, which he described as 'a ghastly mess now, a good idea ruined'. When Abraham Lincoln met Harriet Beecher Stowe he is reported to have said he was impressed to meet the woman whose little book started such a great war. By that standard, and Orwell's, *Nineteen Eighty-Four* is one of the seminal 'Good Bad Books' of all time.

The literary journey that led to this was an arduous one. To read the initial pages of *Burmese Days* today is to be quite taken aback by how poor they are. We are introduced at once to a kind of Ian Fleming villain, the bloated and saturnine Burmese magistrate U Po Kyin, who might as well be depicted as a fat spider sitting at the centre of a web of intrigue. His menacing style is of the 'Oriental' variety; he says things like: 'How little you understand the European mind, Ko Ba Sein!' Hardly has this clanking effect been produced before we are transported, in the company of Flory, to the Englishman's club, where we meet the noxious Ellis, a foul-mouthed local business type. It is not enough that this man speaks at once and grossly about 'that pot-bellied greasy little sod of a nigger doctor' — Flory's only friend. We are further informed, but by the narrator, that Ellis is 'one of those Englishmen — common, unfortunately — who should never be allowed to set foot in the East'. This is telling us what to think, and with a bony elbow in the ribs for additional emphasis.

How, then, does the novel succeed in overcoming this clumsiness and naiveté? Partly by the sheer sincerity of its prose. We are brought to feel that Flory is not feigning his disgust at the way his fellow-Englishmen behave; that his outrage is authentic, his friendship with the lonely little Indian doctor is genuine, and the existence of a suppressed finer feeling something more than a pose. The very title *Burmese Days* is an implied parody of the bluff and hearty memoirs and recollections of the period and place — 'With Rod and Gun up the Irawaddy' etc. — and one of the discriminations employed by Orwell/Flory is a slight but untrained feeling for literature as opposed to the *Blackwood's* magazine and *Punch*-browsing philistinism of the club members. The influence of Conrad can be felt, both in the physical descriptions and in the pervading ennui which can be the antechamber to despair. As is customary with Orwell, there are very few jokes and they are extremely dry. Dr Veeraswami has a ridiculous image for his dreadful foe U Po Kyin — the crocodile that 'strikes always at the weakest spot' — and this absurd repetition contributes something to undoing the Fu Manchu cliché of the original portrayal. Flory's servant, represented as a sort of Oriental negation of Jeeves (when he says 'I have done so' he means that he may or will do so, not that he is three moves ahead of his master), is also described as 'one of the obscure martyrs of bigamy'.

The treatment of race and sex is quite advanced for its time, and quite candid, too. Flory is made to listen to a silly and nasty diatribe from Elizabeth against Eurasians: 'I've heard that half-castes always inherit what's worst in both races'. . . and replies: 'Well, they've all got fathers, you see.' This deft, moral placing of responsibility for the miscegenation so loudly abhorred by whites is accompanied by some fairly graphic scenes in which 'exploitation' of the natives in the sexual sense is shown as the counterpart to the more accustomed use of the term. The idea of 'repression' also presents itself in this dual sense; a thing to keep your eye on, as Orwell might have said, is the continual occurrence of fawning, cringing, begging and other forms of abject and debasing conduct. This element of the master–slave relationship, first noticed with a shudder by Orwell when he was at boarding school, was to be reserved and refined for a later purpose. So was a related subject — the tendency of humans to betray one another for shameful or cowardly reasons, as Flory betrays the pathetic Veeraswami when the inevitable choice presents itself.

Otherwise, *Burmese Days* is a white-man's-grave novel masquerading fairly plausibly as an anti-colonial one and the agencies of self-destruction are, as ever, alcohol, heat and women. The feminists are given another drubbing even in this unlikely locale; Elizabeth Lackersteen's mother is described as 'an incapable, half-baked, vapouring, self-pitying woman who shirked all the normal duties of life on the strength of sensibilities which she did not possess. After messing about for years with such things as Women's Suffrage and Higher Thought . . .' In common with some other critics of imperialism, Orwell was inclined to blame white women for making the men even more racist than they were to begin with, and for importing schoolmarmish hysterias of rape and pillage into an already fraught situation, and for being hard on the servants. But the animus clearly lay deeper than that.

Driven to suicide by booze and by unpardonable and unbearable thoughts of Elizabeth's defloration by another man, Flory first shoots his dog in the head and then, noticing the mess this makes, decides not to be found that way and so shoots himself in the heart. This instant of last-minute solipsism — observing the practical etiquette of life while hurtling towards death — recalls the superbly observed irrelevance of the condemned Burmese convict's gesture in Orwell's essay 'A Hanging':

And once, in spite of the men who gripped him by each shoulder, he stepped slightly aside to avoid a puddle on the path.

It is curious, but till that moment I had never realised what it means to destroy a healthy, conscious man. When I saw the prisoner step aside to avoid the puddle, I saw the mystery, the unspeakable wrongness, of cutting a life short when it is in full tide.

Recall Mrs Leavis's lethal judgment that Orwell's novels are failures while 'his equivalent works in non-fiction are stimulating'. Nothing in *Burmese Days* rises to the level of 'A Hanging', or of 'Shooting an Elephant', or indeed of some other shorter journalistic glimpses of reality in colonial Burma.

For the next three novels, much the same holds true. Orwell's account of the hop-pickers in *Down and Out in Paris and London* is greatly preferable to the one given in *A Clergyman's Daughter*. Drabness and misery are more expertly evoked in *The Road to Wigan Pier* than in *Keep the Aspidistra Flying*. The more fully realized *Coming Up for Air* is a reworking of certain themes more fully treated in the essays: suburban complacency, political sloganizing, the sense of impending and terrifying war. Its relative success as a novel is in the profound exploration of nostalgia, to employ the word in its original sense as an incurable longing for home. (It is fascinating to learn that Orwell wrote this melancholy hymn to the Edwardian Thames Valley while he was living in Morocco, fascinating in the same way as the discovery that P. G. Wodehouse wrote *Joy in the Morning* while interned by the

Nazis in a disused lunatic asylum in Poland. Given the title *Coming Up for Air*, it is touching also to reflect that Orwell voyaged to North Africa in a vain attempt to heal his lungs.)

A Clergyman's Daughter is a finer novel than Orwell believed it to be. True, it begins in a rather banal fashion, with an alarm clock giving off a 'nagging feminine clamour'. True, we find that Dorothy has her signature physical blemish ('her left forearm was spotted with tiny red marks') just as Flory has the blaze on his cheek, George Bowling has his vast belly, Gordon Comstock his dwarfish stature and Winston Smith his varicose ulcer. Yet as the action unfolds, we are given quite a tender and sympathetic portrait of a second-rate but conscientious person, as she struggles both to remain sane and functional and — which is ostensibly more important to her — to retain her hold upon her Christian faith. Everything around her seems to be a sign or a portent (a sure symptom in itself of an impending crack-up) and each invocation of a trusty text or verse brings its own distressful awareness of diminishing returns. Boxer the carthorse is not more faithful than Dorothy in her compensating mantra of self-sacrifice: 'I will work harder.' She cannot bend, but she can break. When the break comes, it is complete.

It can't be said that Orwell exactly thinks himself into the role of an amnesiac and derelict woman. There are one or two moments, however, when he observes the good novelist's rule of letting the reader's imagination supply the missing passage. ('It was always women that she begged from, of course. She did once try begging from a man — but only once.') For the rest, he shows himself in debt as

ever to Dickens, both in the unoriginal form of the ghastly
school-monger Mrs Creevy and the slightly more inventive
form of the old roué Mr Warburton, who is a kind of un-
ethical Cheeryble or hyperactive Barkis. There is, in the
'live' conversation of the losers in Trafalgar Square at midnight, a distant echo of Joyce:

> Mr Tallboys (*stage curate-wise*): The wages of sin is kippers.
> Ginger: Don't breathe in my face, Deafie. I can't bleeding
>   stand it.
> Charlie (*in his sleep*): Charles-Wisdom-drunk-and-
>   incapable-drunk?-yes-six-shillings-move-on-*next*!
> Dorothy (*on Mrs McElligot's bosom*): Oh, joy, joy!

There is also — Orwell allowed himself this quite often — a
moment of identification with the overseer as opposed to the
underdog. Dorothy, for all her best efforts, finds herself looking at the children under her care in the same way as Flory
sometimes saw the Burmese: 'But there were other times
when her nerves were more on edge than usual, and when
she looked round at the score of silly little faces, grinning or
mutinous, and found it possible to hate them.'

Orwell's capacity for vicarious identification with the boss
as well as the bossed has been too little remarked upon, and
was to serve him well later on. In the result, though, he confined himself to sketching the mental and social confines of
Dorothy's own prison, and to emphasizing that these, partly
consisting of mind-wrought manacles, were also socially determined. Not since Osbert Sitwell's *Before The Bombardment*

had any novelist so pitilessly itemized the alternatives for single women without capital in a stratified and ossified society: grudgingly paid 'companionship' to some domineering older lady; domestic service; skivvying for the church; inculcating orthodoxy into wretched schoolchildren — or madness and the charity ward. We might at least recall how recently this picture ceased to be realistic.

Half-way through Dorothy's travail she is reminded of 'a favourite saying of Mr Warburton's, that if you took I Corinthians, chapter thirteen, and in every verse wrote "money" instead of "charity", the chapter had ten times as much meaning as before'. This profane rendition in fact appears on the title page of *Keep the Aspidistra Flying*, which shows what a relatively small stock of fictional ideas Orwell had to draw upon. (At rock-bottom, Gordon Comstock lands in a bug-infested tenement just off Lambeth Cut — the same address at which Dorothy fetched up.) Once again in this novel we are in the frowsty world of futility and inanition, penny-pinching and oppressive respectability. Once again, dreams of escape are vain. There is a description of drinking beer against the clock that might have been a model for Alan Sillitoe's *Saturday Night and Sunday Morning*, and a single joke makes its strictly rationed appearance. ('The principal event of the day was when the hearse drove up to the undertaker's establishment next door. This had a faint interest for Gordon, because the dye was wearing off one of the horses and it was assuming by degrees a curious purplish-brown shade.') At the beginning of the book, Gordon's puny volume of poems is likened to a row of foetuses in individual jars, the very image of the sterile and abortive. Redeeming this by means of a hastily conceived pregnancy is not Orwell's most innovative fictional resolution. However, in the glimpses of the world of advertising — the slick careerist world from which Gordon is in flight — there is a prefiguration of the later *Room at the Top* style, critical of Madison Avenue values, that became such a theme in the British culture of the late 1950s and early 60s, and is especially associated, for us, with the late Dennis Potter.

Coming Up for Air is still read as a masterly evocation of an English Edwardian rural childhood, with its yearning for a time of peace and, perhaps more important, a time of security. It may also be the origin of a well-known saying: 'Has it ever struck you that there's a thin man inside every fat man, just as they say there's a statue inside every block of stone?' George Bowling is everything Orwell was not — stout and ruddy, mutinously married with children, relatively apolitical and phlegmatic. As *homme moyen sensuel,* however, he registers the signals of impending world war and catastrophe. The book belongs to the period when Orwell himself was fatally divided in his mind over the question of whether war or Nazism presented the greater danger, and it would be interesting to know whether, as he wrote Bowling's internal monologues on the subject, he realized how grandly he kept contradicting himself. In a suggestive moment, however, Bowling decides that it's not the war he dreads so much as 'the after-war. The world we're going down into, the kind of hate-world, slogan-world. The coloured shirts, the barbed wire, the rubber truncheons. The secret cells where the electric light burns night and day, and the detectives watching you while you sleep.' Underlying this is an attachment to nature, which is everywhere facing assault and desecration: 'It's the only thing worth having, and we don't want it.' In the end, Bowling knows more about politics and ideas than, to stay in character, he really should. But as one fat Englishman, longing for a time that probably never was, he has worn surprisingly well.

These four pre-war efforts constitute a sort of amateur throat-clearing. It was *Animal Farm* which, as Orwell later wrote, 'was the first book in which I tried, with full consciousness of what I was doing, to fuse political purpose and artistic purpose into one whole'. The lasting success of the undertaking lies in its beautiful simplicity and brevity, but also in its unusual lightness of touch. There is a joke at the very beginning of the animals' revolution, when 'some hams hanging in the kitchen were taken out for burial'. Since the opening picture is not one of unrelieved gloom, the gradual emergence of a tragedy assumes a due proportion. The analogies have charm; each beast is well-cast in its respective role, and well-named into the bargain.

As an allegory the story has one enormous failure: the persons of Lenin and Trotsky are combined into one, or, it might even be truer to say, there is no Lenin-pig at all. Such a stupendous omission cannot have been accidental (especially since it recurs in *Nineteen Eighty-Four*, where there is only Big Brother on the one hand and Emmanuel Goldstein on the other). Orwell in his essays was fond of saying that both Lenin and Trotsky bore some responsibility for Stalinism; by eliding this thought — as well as the difference between the February and October revolutions — he may have been subconsciously catering to the needs of tragedy. The aims and principles of the Russian revolution are given face-value credit throughout; this is a revolution betrayed, not a revolution that is monstrous from its inception. The details are sometimes uncannily exact, from the fate of the Third International to Stalin's eventual compromise — via Moses the fabulist raven — with the Russian Orthodox Church. The abolition of the song 'Beasts of England' is given in slightly anachronistic time, but the way in which the animals sing it when they realize what the pigs have done, 'three times over — very tunefully, but slowly and mournfully, in a way they had never sung it before', is intended to wrench the heart. Those displaced Ukrainians, living in camps after the Second World War, who first applied to Orwell to translate and distribute the book were hearing a distant melody of 'The Internationale' that had once meant something to them.

A phrase much used by Communist intellectuals of the period was 'the great Soviet *experiment*'. That latter word should have been enough in itself to put people on their guard. To turn a country into a laboratory is to give ample warning of inhumanity. So queasy are we about the thought of experiments on living people that we try them out first — on animals. Orwell spoke, perhaps, more truly than he knew when he decided on the title and subtitle of his 'fairy story'.

Another unremarked element of the book, more striking with the passage of time, is its prescience. Everybody remembers that by the closing sentence, the frightened and famished beasts are unable to distinguish between the men and the pigs. But, in the scene which culminates with this line, Napoleon has actually invited Mr Jones to return, and changed the name of the enterprise back into 'Manor Farm'. Trotsky in exile predicted that the Stalinist bureaucrats would one day sell off the socialized property that they had expropriated, and go into business on their own account. So, not only did Orwell produce a brilliant satire on the self-negation of Communism, he even anticipated its eventual terminus in a robber-baron Mafia capitalist state. Counter-revolutions devour their children, too.

But all of this was prologue to the near-desperate race-against-time achievement of *Nineteen Eighty-Four*, a novel which created physical and mental fear in the first people to read it. (Orwell's publisher Fredric Warburg wrote, when he had recovered from the shock, that 'here is a study in pessimism unrelieved, except by the thought that, if a man can conceive "1984", he can also will to avoid it'.) Into these *noir* pages Orwell poured everything he had learned, heaping agony on misery on defeat, and synthesizing much of his study of literature as well as his condensed and concentrated experience as a journalist. In commending Dickens, he once wrote that the creator of David Copperfield and Sidney Carton had the face of a man who was 'generously angry'. He never quite attained to the peak of generosity in his own fiction, and *Nineteen Eighty-Four* is more like rage than anger, rage against the dying of the light. From the idea of experiments on animals he moves, in the frigid and toneless words of the Party boss O'Brien, to the Party neurologists working on the abolition of the orgasm and the Party definition of power as 'tearing human minds to pieces and putting them together again in new shapes of your own choosing'.

Many have noticed the similarity between aspects of the book and Evgeny Zamyatin's *We*, a Russian dystopia of a slightly earlier period. Isaac Deutscher even alleged falsely that there was plagiarism involved, but Orwell had recommended the book in print, had urged Fredric Warburg to publish it, and had written to its translator Gleb Struve as early as 1944 saying: 'I am interested in that kind of book, and even keep making notes for one myself that may get written sooner or later.' (Struve later became the translator of Mandelstam.) In truth, the idea that two and two make five, for instance, was suggested by multiple sources. Stalin's propagandists were fond of saying that they completed the first Five Year Plan in four years; this was sometimes rendered for the simple-minded as 2+2=5. Sterne's *Tristram Shandy* has a comparable moment of official juggling with numbers, as does Dostoyevsky's *Notes From Underground*.

Nineteen Eighty-Four is the only English contribution to the literature of twentieth-century totalitarianism, able to stand comparison with Silone and Koestler and Serge and Solzhenitsyn. It is a summa of what Orwell learned about terror and conformism in Spain, what he learned about servility and sadism at school and in the Burma police, what he discovered about squalor and degradation in *The Road to Wigan Pier*, what he learned about propaganda and falsity in decades of polemical battles. It contains absolutely no jokes. It is the first and only time that his efforts as a novelist rise to the level of his essays.

Let me give a trivial illustration. In 'Such, Such Were the Joys', a stupid English schoolboy does poorly in an examination and receives a terrific thrashing from the headmaster, after which he comments ruefully that he wishes he'd had the thrashing before the exam. The young Orwell notices how 'contemptible' this remark is. And here is the abject figure of Parsons, complete with khaki shorts and schoolboy manner, in the cellars of the Ministry of Love:

> 'Of course I'm guilty!' cried Parsons with a servile glance at the telescreen. 'You don't think the Party would arrest an innocent man, do you? . . . Between you and me, old man, I'm glad they got me before it went any further. Do you know what I'm going to say to them when I go up before the tribunal? "Thank you," I'm going to say, "thank you for saving me before it was too late." '

Parsons then has an infantile and disgusting moment on the cell latrine, the horrid pungency of which derives from numerous prisons frequented by Orwell himself, both as guard and as inmate. The sense of stifling and fetid enclosure is more terrifying than some later fictional attempts to describe hell, because it is more hermetic even than *No Exit* and even more willing to face the possibility that it is the prisoners themselves who help to bar the doors. The will to command and to dominate is one thing, but the will to obey and be prostrate is a deadly foe as well. At one point in a short earlier article, Orwell asked himself if decency and powerlessness were inversely related. Nobody has ever made this point more forcibly than he does in *Nineteen Eighty-Four*, just as nobody since Dostoyevsky has come so close to reading the mind of the Grand Inquisitor. With a part of themselves, humans relish cruelty and war and absolute capricious authority, are bored by civilized and humane pursuits and understand only too well the latent connection between sexual repression and orgiastic vicarious collectivized release. Some regimes have been popular not in spite of their irrationality and cruelty, but because of it. There will always be Trotskys and Goldsteins and even Winston Smiths, but it must be clearly understood that the odds are overwhelmingly against them, and that as with Camus's rebel, the crowd will yell with joy to see them dragged to the scaffold. This long and steady look into the void was Orwell's apotheosis of 'the power of facing'.

9

Deconstructing the Post-modernists
Orwell and Transparency

Even more than the deceptively simple question of his 'Englishness', Orwell's posthumous standing as a representative of truth-telling, objectivity and verification continues to keep his ideas in play. I mention this in the same breath as the English question because, superficially at any rate, there exists an intellectual chasm between the 'Anglo-Saxon' tradition and the efforts made by 'Continental' theorists to explain the world.

In the last three decades of the twentieth century, Anglo-Saxondom was itself extensively colonized by the schools of post-modernism and 'deconstruction' of texts, by the ideas of the *nouveau roman* and by those who regarded 'objectivity' as an ideology. On the campuses of British and American universities, the works of Foucault and Derrida enjoyed something more than a fashion. On the Left, Louis Althusser's attempt to recreate Communism by abstract thought was probably the last exhalation of the idea, terminating in his own insanity and by what I once rather heartlessly called his application for the Electric Chair of Philosophy at the École Abnormale. While among the more affectless and detached ('post-modernism' consisting in essence of the view that nothing would ever again happen for the first time), Jean Baudrillard won golden opinions for such propositions as the fictional nature of the Gulf War, a war which, he 'ironically' suggested, had not 'really' taken place.

In confrontations between this cult of the arcane and the 'virtual' and its critics, the name of George Orwell kept insistently surfacing. A new stage in the argument was opened by Professor Alan Sokal, who in 1997 submitted a satirical article to the journal *Social Text*. The essay maintained that scientific procedures of testability and experiment were themselves culturally produced or constructed, and possessed no independent validity. On seeing his preposterous submission accepted and published by the editors, Professor Sokal revealed the hoax. From then on, the debate between the rival academic tendencies took on a slightly rancorous tone. So much so that in the January 2000 issue of the academic journal *Lingua Franca*, Professor James Miller offered an overview of the scene under the incendiary title: 'Is Bad Writing Necessary?'

The question was not without its point. Scholars like Judith Butler at the University of California had been arguing that 'linguistic transparency' was a deception, compelling intellectuals to confine themselves to the demotic and hampering the capacity 'to think the world more radically'.

Those who took this position — Gayatri Spivak notable among them — tended to cite Theodor Adorno. Those who opposed it — Noam Chomsky, for example — commonly used Orwell's insistence on plain *contestable* speech as one of their critical resources. Contrasting Adorno and Orwell, Professor Miller came up with some similarities, some antitheses and some unexpected syntheses.

Adorno suspected 'plain words' of being the vehicles of consensus because, as he phrased it in his classic *Minima Moralia*, those engaged in the practice were not as free as they supposed. 'Only what they do not need first to understand, they consider understandable; only the word coined by commerce, and really alienated, touches them as familiar. Few things contribute so much to the demoralization of the intellectuals. Those who would escape it must recognize the advocates of communicability as traitors to what they communicate.' Judith Butler took this as — if she will forgive the expression — her text. Actually, as well as its easy intelligibility, there is little enough in this with which Orwell would have disagreed. He was fond of drawing attention to the surreptitious importing of received opinions, through political slogans and advertising jingles, and the way in which people fell into the trap of expressing conventional thoughts that did not really belong to them:

> When you think of something abstract you are more inclined to use words from the start, and unless you make a conscious effort to prevent it, the existing dialect will come rushing in and do the job for you, at the expense of blurring or even changing your meaning.

And indeed, Adorno returned the compliment by writing that: 'Where there is something that needs to be said, indifference to literary form always indicates dogmatization of content.'

The difference, however, lay in their respective attitudes to the speakers as well as the speech. Appalled by the demagogic populist element in modern despotism, Adorno felt that men of culture and refugees like himself should be unapologetic intellectual elitists. By way of self-contradiction, he also maintained that 'lucidity, objectivity, and concise precision' were little more than 'ideologies', 'invented' by 'editors and then writers for their own accommodation'. Well, every form of discourse is in some way invented, just as every position including the ostensibly neutral is in the last instance ideological. But for Orwell, a common language with accepted and mutually understood rules was an indispensable condition for an open democracy. (I cannot prove this from textual evidence, but there are enough admiring references in his prose to the Protestant Revolution to make me sure that he connected this to the old struggle to have the Bible translated into the vernacular, instead of being 'The Book' of a Latinate Catholic 'Inner Party'.) 'Prose literature as we know it,' he wrote, 'is the product of rationalism, of the Protestant centuries, of the autonomous individual.'

Stylistically, the two men had a certain amount in common. They liked to open or close their essays with arresting generalizations or paradoxes (Adorno: 'In psychoanalysis nothing is true except the exaggerations'; 'Normality is death'. Orwell: 'Autobiography is not to be trusted unless it reveals something disgraceful'; 'Freedom is slavery'). Orwell had not read Heidegger or Husserl, but he would have been very absorbed by Adorno's views of 'the authoritarian personality'. The two had a radically discrepant attitude towards the seductions of the passive voice or the impersonal noun; Orwell would have well understood what Adorno was driving at when he wrote: 'Topsyturviness perpetuates itself: domination is propagated by the dominated', but would himself have stated it more bluntly and actively, probably offering an actual example.

There was much loose talk in the 1980s and 90s of the dichotomy between '*langue*' and '*parole*', of the work of Lacan and Saussure, in defining the structuralist paradigm. *Langue* tries to determine matters in advance, *parole* offers a chance to interpolate a word or two. Reviewing the dispute, Perry Anderson remarked that 'even the greatest writers, whose genius has influenced whole cultures, have typically altered the language very little'. Orwell is not the exception that Anderson had in mind, yet he did bring a freshet of new political terms into the language, and did alter the way in which even relatively unlettered people became aware of the power of it.

Adorno was an accomplished theorist of music, with an interest in the atonal work of his friend Alban Berg, and he used the analogy of music to write about the legacy of Nietzsche, who cared nothing for public opinion and who 'wondered whether anyone was listening when he sang to himself "a secret barcarole"'. Who, inquired Adorno, could complain 'if even the freest of free spirits no longer write for an

imaginary posterity . . . but only for the dead God?' In the
extremity in which Orwell wrote *Nineteen Eighty-Four* —
the original title of which was, suggestively enough, 'The
Last Man in Europe' — he too knew this feeling of being
the last Roman waiting for the barbarians. Winston Smith
addresses his doomed text thus:

> To the future or to the past, to a time when thought is
> free, when men are different from one another and do not
> live alone — to a time when truth exists and what is done
> cannot be undone:
>
>> From the age of uniformity, from the age of solitude,
>> from the age of Big Brother, from the age of doublethink
>> — greetings!

Here is a gesture to stand comparison with Adorno's image of
Nietzsche 'leaving behind messages in bottles on the flood of
barbarism bursting on Europe'. But Smith, though he does
not mention Newspeak in his litany, is clear that one does not
need a new language with which to oppose doublethink and
lies. What one needs is a pure speech that means what it says,
and that can be subjected to refutation in its own terms. This
will very often be an *old* speech, organically connected to the
ancient truths preserved and transmitted by literature.

In his own version of Smith's despair and internal exile,
Adorno lost faith even in that. 'No poetry after Auschwitz', as
he famously said in a statement that is somehow as profound
as it is absurd. Neither man would have believed that, only a
half-century or so after the Hitler–Stalin pact, every major

city in Europe would be able to claim a free press and a free university. This outcome owes something to both men but more, one suspects, to the Englishman than to the Frankfurt theorist.

More than any one thing, the 'Continental' school repudiates the empiricist view of the a priori: the notion that non-theoretical facts are simply *there*, awaiting discovery. Of course, no English philosopher really held such an opinion; the work of Berkeley and Hume is more concerned with deciding upon what is factual and what is not, and with the procedures for determining this. It may one day seem strange that, in our own time of extraordinary and revolutionary innovation in the physical sciences, from the human genome to the Hubble telescope, so many 'radicals' spent so much time casting casuistic doubt on the concept of verifiable truth. But in the field of fictional narrative more latitude is permissible, and once again Orwell was the touchstone in a celebrated test of this.

The French novelist Claude Simon, grand practitioner of the *nouveau roman*, won the Nobel Prize for Literature in 1985, in part for his 1981 novel *The Georgics*, which bears the loosest possible relationship to Virgil, except for its invocation of the abstract muse of capital H 'History'. The 'George' of the title turns out to be George Orwell, whose account of the Spanish Civil War M. Simon announced, in an interview given to *The Review of Contemporary Fiction*, to have been 'faked from the very first sentence'.

The very first sentence of *Homage to Catalonia* reads: 'In the Lenin Barracks in Barcelona, the day before I joined the militia, I saw an Italian militiaman standing in front of the officers' table.' To this, Simon responds with a burst of what he supposes to be withering scorn, saying that if any should find:

> after analysing it, that this sentence is innocent (what it says, and above all what it carefully omits to say) it is because they are singularly ignorant of the political circumstances in Barcelona at that time, and, in general, of the circumstances in revolutionary movements in Europe at that same period. I shall restrict myself to informing them that one did not just wander casually into Republican Spain at that time, and that if there did exist in Barcelona something called the 'Lenin Barracks' (or rather a 'Cuartel Lenin'), there was also, not far away, 'Cuartel Karl Marx', and another invoking the name of Bakunin.

One might pause to note that Simon, who elsewhere favours an entirely relativist attitude to questions of historical 'fact', is here insisting on strict and literal accuracy. But he leaves open the question of whether or not there 'really' was such a place as the Lenin Barracks, while suggesting that Orwell gave an impression of complete indifference to factional politics in Catalonia. As it happens, we are in the same position as the one in which Winston Smith finds himself early in *Nineteen Eighty-Four*. We possess — and unlike Smith, are at liberty to reproduce — a photograph of the Lenin Barracks in Barcelona, with Orwell mustered under a POUM banner outside it. Is this a sufficient refutation?

Probably not, from M. Simon's point of view. The whole of Part Four of his novel is an obsessive reworking of the action of *Homage to Catalonia*, rendered closer to the writer's desire in an attempt to show that the original 'author' could not really have seen what he claimed to have witnessed. The contradiction arises, according to the not-easily-summarized M. Simon:

> Either because he takes certain facts for granted (his past: the education he received in the aristocratic college of Eton, the five years he spends in the imperial police in the Indies, his sudden resignation, the ascetic life he inflicts upon himself afterwards, going to live in a depressed district in the East End, working as a dishwasher in Paris restaurants, his first literary efforts, his political opinions), or because, for one reason or another, he passes over his own motivations in silence (for example the steps he takes on his first return from the front to join the faction to which he has up till then been opposed as soon as he realizes that, being about to gain power, it is more likely to afford him better than any other the opportunity to achieve his aims, even if it means joining in against his former comrades in the repression of which he will himself be a victim).

I should perhaps add here that this translation is produced by self-described devotees of M. Simon and thus that formulations like 'it is more likely to afford him better than any other' are not attributable to malice. Punctuation is similar in both languages; it is on his own initiative that M. Simon

often goes for more than a page without a full stop. At any
rate it is clear that the author, though his advertised purpose
is to demonstrate the impossibility of rendering an objective
account, feels abundant confidence in his own ability to
guess the mental processes and motives of someone he has
never met.

Very often, people embarking on such guesswork make
the vulgar assumption that the lower the motives, the more
likely they are to be authentic. So M. Simon proceeds, after
more borrowing from the original, to say:

> In order to carry conviction, he tries (pretends?) to stick
> to facts (only later on will he try to write a commentary
> on them), livening his account with just enough local
> colour to prevent it from having the dryness of a straight-
> forward report, giving it more persuasiveness, credibility,
> through several notations of those details, those eyewit-
> ness aspects, which every competent journalist knows
> constitute the best guarantees of authenticity of a piece of
> reporting, especially when they are inserted into a form of
> writing which presents itself as neutral (he has recourse to
> short sentences, he eschews wherever possible value-
> loaded adjectives and generally anything which might ap-
> pear to give the appearance of a partisan or tendentious
> interpretation of events, for all the world as if he had not
> been closely involved in them but had been a dispassion-
> ate witness concerned only with gathering information).

Again, one hardly knows whether to laugh or to weep ('anything which might appear to give the appearance . . .'; the

sinister import of short sentences; the sheer dishonesty of es-
chewing value-loaded adjectives). And that is only at the
style. The crucial point, as I hope I helped to show on pp.
67–70 earlier is that *Homage to Catalonia* in fact *can* be read
as a piece of objective reportage, even though it is laughable
for M. Simon to suggest that it ever posed as nonpartisan.
The claims made are subject to verification, and are body-
guarded with warnings about the author's own subjectivity.
However, it turns out that those prisoners *were* framed, that a
covert Stalinist direction of events *can* be ascertained, that
there *is* value to personal eyewitness testimony. And it would
be feeble to suggest that these were presented as 'independent'
pre-theoretical truths, waiting around to be discovered by disinterested inquiry. On the contrary, they were conclusions
formed in, and by means of, a protracted and difficult struggle. Perhaps Orwell stumbled on the near impossible: the
synthesis of the empiricist dialectic.

M. Simon had himself been in Spain, though fighting
on the side of the Stalintern forces, and must at some point
have believed that 'History' did indeed have a point and a
direction, and was indeed on 'his' side. Subsequently lapsing in that belief — though not in his attachment to the
USSR — he opted for indiscriminate relativist promiscuity,
where nothing can be taken as certain except the bad faith
of those with whom he disagrees. The award of the Nobel
Prize to such a shady literary enterprise is a minor scandal,
reflecting the intellectual rot which had been spread by
pseudo-intellectuals. Their supposedly lofty preference for
the arbitrary, the contingent and the random did little to
mask their own private suspicion that established facts

would not place their own theories — their own subjective dogmas, actually — in a very forgiving light.

This fallacy in so-called 'critical theory' and its literary counterparts is arguably a lethal one. Adorno hated the crass materialism of American journalism, and rightly suspected that its claim to provide 'facts full in the face' was boastful and empty. He overbalanced this criticism by comparing it to 'the form and timbre of the command issued under Fascism by the dumb to the silent'. But 'comprehensibility to the most stupid', as he put it, has advantages over condescension. A lie can be detected even by the simplest folk; would Adorno (I say nothing of Simon) have had it otherwise? As Professor Miller pointed out, if the critical theorists are right, and a linguistic 'retention of strangeness is the only antidote to estrangement', then what occurs when the 'new' language becomes current and intelligible? Must it not lose its ability to safeguard 'advanced' thinking? Orwell's wager, in spite of some lapses into pessimism, was that the profane were well able to understand the language of the temple, and thus to penetrate the supposed secrets of authority. He did of course deploy a 'subjective' and unquantifiable tool, something that cannot be taught or inherited, but the old name for this X-factor is intellectual honesty.

10

In Conclusion

'Objectivity' though in practice as unattainable as infinity, is useful in the same way, at least as a fixed point of theoretical reference. A knowledge of one's own subjectivity is necessary in order even to contemplate the 'objective'; our modern idiom slightly mangles the work of Heisenberg and Godel in order to convey this awareness. Terms such as 'neutral', 'detached', let alone 'fair-minded', 'disinterested' or 'evenhanded' do not all convey the same meaning; they are merely aestheticized forms of the same subjective aspiration.

The disputes and debates and combats in which George Orwell took part are receding into history, but the manner in which he conducted himself as writer and participant has a reasonable chance of remaining as a historical example of its own. I first struck across his writing at about the same period that I encountered the poetry of W. H. Auden, and it has subsequently grieved me that the quarrel between the two men makes it impossible to esteem them as allies, or as co-authors of equivalent moral clarity. This is Orwell's fault: his attack on Auden is one of the few thuggish episodes in his prose, and is also related to his unexamined and philistine prejudice against homosexuality. But this depressing episode has its redeeming sequel, as I shall try to show.

In May 1937 — the very worst month in the battle between the Spanish Republic and the deadly metastasis of Stalin's regime within Spanish institutions — Auden published a long and beautiful poem entitled, simply, 'Spain'. The publication was not without its propaganda dimension; the poem first appeared as a shilling pamphlet with proceeds going to a Popular Front-organization 'medical aid' charity. However, in form and content the verses summon the idea of Spain itself ('that arid square, that fragment nipped off from hot/Africa, soldered so crudely to inventive Europe'); the place it then held in the hearts and minds of thinking people ('Our thoughts have bodies; the menacing shapes of our fever/Are precise and alive'); and finally the agony experienced by those non-violent intellectuals who had decided to abandon neutrality and, suppressing misgiving, endorse the use of force in self-defence:

> To-day the deliberate increase in the chances of death,
> The conscious acceptance of guilt in the necessary murder;
>   To-day the expending of powers
> On the flat ephemeral pamphlet and the boring meeting.

It is hard to imagine it being put better: the fascist poets and writers had exulted in violence and cruelty and domineering rhetoric, celebrating death and denigrating the intellect, while their opponents gathered resolve reluctantly yet with mounting determination. This was not at all Orwell's reading of the poem. In two articles, one of them written for *The Adelphi* in 1938 and another more celebrated under the title 'Inside The Whale', he took venomous aim at the above stanza in particular. It was, he sneered:

> a sort of tabloid picture of a day in the life of a 'good party man'. In the morning a couple of political murders, a ten-minutes' interlude to stifle 'bourgeois' remorse, and then a hurried luncheon and a busy afternoon and evening chalking walls and distributing leaflets. All very edifying. But notice the phrase 'necessary murder'. It could only be written by a person to whom murder is at most a *word*. Personally I would not speak so lightly of murder . . . The Hitlers and Stalins find murder necessary, but . . . they don't speak of it as murder; it is 'liquidation', 'elimination' or some other soothing phrase. Mr Auden's brand of amoralism is only possible if you are the kind of person who is always somewhere else when the trigger is pulled.

The laden sarcasm here is as gross as the cheapness of the argument. Who can possibly have thought that terms (not phrases) like 'liquidation' or 'elimination' were 'soothing'? By giving the word 'murder' its rightful name, Auden was precisely *declining* to use the sort of euphemism that Orwell elsewhere found so despicable. His 'brand of amoralism' consisted in a sincere attempt to overcome essentially pacifist scruples, and to be candid about the consequences.

We do not know for certain how much Orwell's excoriation weighed with Auden, but in 1939 he revised 'Spain' to delete all allusions to such moral dilemmas, and by the 1950s he had made sure that the poem, together with some others of the period, could not be anthologized under his name. This is in several ways a great pity: it suggests the mentality of an auto-da-fé and it also tears from its proper context a haunting phrase which still resounds in literary memory. The phrase is 'History to the defeated', and it occurs at the close of the poem, where Auden says: 'We are left alone with our day, and the time is short, and/History to the defeated/May say alas but cannot help or pardon.' He developed a special horror for this formulation, writing later that: 'To say this is to equate goodness with success. It would have been bad enough if I had ever held this wicked doctrine, but that I should have stated it simply because it sounded to me rhetorically effective is quite inexcusable.' Perhaps he was being too harsh on himself; few if any readers have interpreted the lines as a ruthless Hegelian equation of history (or 'History') with victory. Rather, the lines acquire their power from a somewhat remorseful recognition of necessity.

Or so Orwell may have come to believe. In concluding a review of a book by General Wavell in the critical month of December 1940, he wrote, of the preceding First World War:

The thick-necked cavalry generals remained at the top, but the lower–middle classes and the colonies came to the rescue. The thing is happening again, and probably on a much larger scale, but it is happening with desperate slowness and

> *History to the defeated*
> *May say Alas! But cannot alter or pardon.*

He quoted from memory as he often did, but seemed to approve the sentiment as rousing people to see that here was a war which could not be lost. He also seemed to assume that his readers would know the poem, and see the point.

In January 1946, writing an essay which abominated the new fashion for artificial pleasure-resorts, he quoted again, this time from Auden's 'September 1, 1939':

> *The lights must never go out.*
> *The music must always play,*
> *Lest we should see where we are,*
> *Lost in a haunted wood,*
> *Children afraid of the dark*
> *Who have never been happy or good.*

Even when writing 'Inside The Whale' several years earlier, he had apologized to Auden for having described him previously as ' "a sort of gutless Kipling". As criticism this was quite unworthy, indeed it was merely a spiteful remark . . .' And, in preparing to take aim at 'Spain', he had taken care to

observe that 'this poem is one of the few decent things that
have been written about the Spanish war'.

Possibly I am wishful in thinking that elements of atonement and restitution are at work here, and that there is more
at stake than Orwell's shortcomings as a critic of poetry
(which in turn are as nothing when compared to his shortcomings as a poet). But it remains the case that, in an epoch
of extreme yet cynically fluctuating factional loyalism, he
managed *both* to be a consistent and adamant foe of both
Hitler and Stalin, while writing commentaries that tried to
be 'objective' about each of them. Of Hitler he wrote that
while he would gladly kill him, he could not hate him. The
abysmal pathos of the man was all too evident. At the last
moment, he changed the proofs of *Animal Farm* so that the
story would say: 'All the animals, except Napoleon, flung
themselves flat on their bellies.' The original had read 'All the
animals, *including* Napoleon', but Orwell had been assured
by Russian exiles that Stalin had remained in Moscow during the German assault, and he wished to be fair to him.
This is the same Orwell who would not shoot at a Spanish
fascist soldier while the man was running from the latrine
and trying to hold up his trousers; the same Orwell who sac-
rificed the enormous extra bounty of a 'Book of the Month
Club' selection, at a time of extreme financial anxiety, rather
than make some minor suggested alterations to his novel.

If it is true that *le style, c'est l'homme* (a proposition which
the admirers of M. Claude Simon must devoutly hope to be
false) then what we have in the person of George Orwell is
by no means the 'saint' mentioned by V. S. Pritchett and

Anthony Powell. At best it could be asserted, even by an atheist admirer, that he took some of the supposedly Christian virtues and showed how they could be 'lived' without piety or religious belief. It may also be hoped that, to adapt the words of Auden on the death of Yeats, Time itself deals kindly with those who live by and for language. Auden added that Time 'with this strange excuse' would even 'pardon Kipling and his views'. Orwell's 'views' have been largely vindicated by Time, so he need not seek any pardon on that score. But what he illustrates, by his commitment to language as the partner of truth, is that 'views' do not really count; that it matters not what you think, but *how* you think; and that politics are relatively unimportant, while principles have a way of enduring, as do the few irreducible individuals who maintain allegiance to them.